MINIATURE

BONSAI

A Complete Guide to Tiny Bonsai

Hilit Publishing Co., Ltd.

Miniature Bonsai

First English Edition: January 1995

Hilit Publishing Company, Ltd.
8F-1, No. 10, Lane 609, Chung-Hsin Road, Section 5
San Chung City, Taipei Hsien, Taiwan, R.O.C.
FAX: 886-2-999-6526
TEL: 886-2-999-6525

ISBN: 957-629-243-3

Publisher:	Dixson D.S. Sung
Author:	Lin Kuo-cheng
English text:	Brian Klingborg
English Editor:	Lanchi Venator
Photography:	Chao Tien-te, Kao Tsung-chung, Huang Yu-chih
Design:	Yang Chii-Shiunn, Hsu Tien-ming, Sun Fu-mei

Lithographed in Taiwan, R.O.C.

Contents

7   **Bonsai Appreciation**

25   **Basics**

Definition 25

History 28

Key Factors for the Cultivation of Bonsai 32

        sunlight/water/soil/weather/fertilizers/diseases and insects

Styles 40

        single-trunk/twin-trunk/tri-trunk/multi-trunk/
        literati style/cascade style/raft style/
        clinging-to-rock, root-over-rock styles/
        exposed-root style/shari style/group planting

46   **Cultivation**

Propagation 46

        sowing seeds/cutting/layering/grafting/separation/
        collecting from mountains

Shaping 55

        pruning/bud pinching/leaf trimming/wiring

Pots 60

        pot making/choosing pots/potting

Tools 66

Buying Miniature Bonsai 70

75   **Creation**

Trees and Plants 75

        pine/juniper/Chinese sweet gum/maple/elm/Japanese gray-bark elm/banyan/
        azalea/Japanese serissa/bamboo/mulberry/crape myrtle/Fukien tea/fire-thorn/
        herbs/Chinese brake/sweet-rush/cactus

Creating Your Own Bonsai 94

        basics/shaping

Rapid Cultivation 106

Moss 107

109   **Application**

Bonsai Accessories 109

Displaying Bonsai 110

Master Lin Kuo-cheng

Bonsai Appreciation

varnish tree / literati / height:30cm(12 inches) / shell-shaped plate
Chinese elm / twisted-trunk / height:30cm(12 inches) / square earthenware pot
   A windowsill or a table near a window is always a good place for miniature bonsai. Blinds or curtains can be used to sift the sunlight. Miniature bonsai are almost always placed indoors.

trident maple / cascade / length:13cm
(5 inches) / tall red earthenware pot
Japanese flowering quince / cascade
length:10cm(4 inches) / earthenware
pot
Taiwan red maple / literati and twin-
trunk / height:58cm (23 inches) oblong
earthenware pot (pot 2.5cm in height)
Although this Taiwan red maple is as
tall as a medium-sized bonsai, it is still
classified as miniature because the pot it
sprouts from is only the size of a
matchbox. In order to cultivate such a
bonsai, you must move the plant to the
small earthenware pot as soon as it
begins to sprout, and as it grows,
continually trim off horizontal branches
so that it grows only in an upward
direction.

Thunberg berberry / tri-trunk height:10cm (4 inches) / earthenware pot
Chinese elm / cascade / length:13cm(5 inches) / tall square pot

The side branches of the Thunberg berberry have delicate leaves and coarse bark, ideal for miniature bonsai. The elm has a strong life force; even a small part of an elm root will grow. The elm in the picture is 2 years old, and was cultivated from a piece of root.

Taiwan trident maple / twisted-trunk / height:18cm(7 inches) / oblong red earthenware pot

A short tree with comparatively large trunk is a common style for miniature bonsai. To form such a tree, one cuts off the upper part of a normal tree and then carefully cultivates the trunk.

willow fir / twin-trunk / height: 33cm(13 inches) / shallow oval earthenware pot

    Japanese willow fir bonsai are usually cultivated by planting branches cut from a tree. The bonsai in the picture is four years old.

trident maple / clinging-to-rock / rock height:6cm (2.5 inches) / shallow oval earthenware pot
star jasmine / root-over-rock height:3cm(1 inch) / oval glazed earthenware pot
black dragon grass / root-over-rock / rock height: 2cm(8 inch) / tall square earthenware pot

    Here are three different root-sticking-to-rock styles. Trident maple has strong roots that cling to rock. Star jasmine has fragile roots that stretch to surround rock and anchor the plant in place. The roots of black dragon grass penetrate loosely structured stone, creating a firm base.

Japanese gray-bark elm / twin-trunk / height:6cm(2.5 inches) / oval red earthenware pot
dwarf bamboo / multi-trunk / height:7cm(2.7 inches) / shallow square earthenware pot
Japanese serissa / raft / height:10cm(4 inches) / shallow oval glazed earthenware pot
bird's nest fern / multi-trunk / height:14cm(6 inches) / handmade earthenware plate
Chinese elm / twisted-trunk / height:11cm(4.5 inches) / handmade earthenware pot

Chinese elm / root-over-rock, twin-trunk / height:14cm(6 inches) / oblong earthenware pot
fragrant maple / literati / height:95cm (38 inches) / shallow square earthenware pot

Bonsai in a literati style are always tall and slender. The literati style is quite simple as compared to that of the bonsai seen on the left.

12

star jasmine / root-over-rock / height: 6cm(2.5 inches) / tall oblong earthenware pot

Star jasmine is an ideal material for creating root-over-rock style bonsai. The tree in the picture was cultivated for two years in a seed bed before being transferred to a pot.

Japanese premna / group planting height(for the highest tree):21cm(8 inches) / shallow oval earthenware pot

In group planting style, the trees should grow as if they are in a forest and a balance should be struck between naturalness and artificiality.

fragrant maple / slanting / height:5cm(2 inches) / handmade earthenware pot

Placing bonsai beside a large French window is a wonderful idea. But the tree should occasionally be set outdoors to take in fresh air.

Taiwan red maple / single-trunk / height: 30cm(12 inches) / red earthenware saucer
Taiwan red maple / twisted-trunk / height: 6cm(2.5 inches) / square white porcelain pot

Placed side by side are an ordinary and a miniature bonsai. The Taiwan red maple, a typical medium-sized bonsai, has been cultivated for 6 years. The miniature bonsai on the right is four years old.

Japanese serissa, varnish tree, ivy, crape myrtle, Japanese azalea / group planting / rock height:17cm(7 inches) / oblong glazed earthenware pot

When group planting, trees should be matched in size and growing speed so as to maintain a harmonious relationship with one another.

pomegranate / twin-trunk / height:12cm(5 inches) / handmade earthenware pot

The trunk of pomegranate tree will naturally twist with the passage of time.

akebia / cascade / horizontal length:18cm (7 inches) / earthenware ewer

akebia / cascade / vertical length:17cm(7 inches) / tall earthenware vase

The two akebia trees pictured here are in fact the same tree. The original bonsai is in the upper right picture; after 1 year's cultivation it attained the appearance depicted to the left.

scouring rush / multi-trunk / height:18cm(7 inches)/ oblong white porcelain pot

Scouring rush usually grows along streams and rivers; it prefers a wet environment. Choose specimens which are short and have dense branches when creating bonsai. Remove withered branches from time to time.

crape myrtle / slanting-trunk / horizontal length:7cm(3 inches) / square red earthenware pot
dwarf stewartia / single-trunk / height:21cm(8 inches)/ handmade earthenware pot

After a long process of cultivation, the color of the crape myrtle bark turns gray-white; the bark of the dwarf stewartia tree turns scarlet. During growth, the trunk of crape myrtle tends to twist but the trunk of dwarf stewartia remains straight.

fir / group planting / height:21cm(8 inches) / handmade glazed earthenware pot

Natural fir is too large a species to make into bonsai. Fir bonsai are the result of advanced cultivation techniques in which natural fir is modified.

Taiwan red maple / exposed-root / height:12cm(5 inches)/ handmade earthenware pot
willow fir / twin-trunk / height:22cm(8 inches) / shallow oval earthenware pot

The bare-trunked and exposed-root red maple looks just like a deer lowering its head. The twin-trunked willow fir is a concrete manifestation of the symbiotic relationship between life and death. One trunk has been stripped of all its bark to allow the other one to grow more quickly.

white dragon grass / multi-trunk / height: 18cm(7 inches) / oblong glazed earthenware pot

scarlet kadsura / twisted-trunk / height: 15cm(6 inches) / round glazed earthenware pot

During growth, plants may sometimes mutate. The color of this white dragon grass has turned completely green, even though the plant it came from was white.

fragrant maple / twisted-trunk / height: 30cm(12 inches) / shallow square earthenware pot

This bonsai was cultivated from a cut side branch of a tree through a process of layering.

Chinese elm / cascade / height:18cm(7 inches) / handmade earthenware pot

(upper right) Chinese pistachio / twin-trunk / height:4cm(1.5 inches) / miniature earthenware bowl
(right) sword fern / multi-trunk / height:14cm (5.5 inches) / earthenware bowl

Both are super-miniature bonsai. To cultivate such small plants, one must lavish attention on them from the very beginning of their cultivation.

bird-lime holly / exposed-root / height: 14cm(5.5 inches) / oblong white porcelain pot

These pictures are of the same bonsai during spring (upper) and winter (lower).

**silver maple / root-over-rock / rock height:6cm(2.5 inches)/
oblong yellow earthenware pot**

Maple trees have thick, egg-shaped leaves. The back of
this type of maple's leaves are silver; thus it is called the
"silver maple."

star jasmine / root-clinging-to-rock / rock height:4cm(1.5 inches) / wide-mouthed round earthenware pot

Star jasmine has many aerial roots that cling to its surroundings, thus making it a good choice for root-clinging-to-rock style bonsai.

silver maple / exposed-root / height:12cm (5 inches) / oblong glazed earthenware pot quadrangular juniper / upright / height: 20cm(8 inches) / square glazed earthenware pot

Quadrangular juniper is a rare species. Its leaves and small twigs change shape during growth, making it an entertaining bonsai to observe.

Basics

Definition

Bonsai combines art with horticulture to produce a form of artistic expression in which one's "canvas" is a living plant. More specifically, bonsai refers to the cultivation of plants that have been transplanted into decorative vessels. While shaped and nurtured by artificial methods, bonsai are nevertheless completely natural objects of art.

It is often assumed that bonsai entails the subjection of innocent plants to horrible forms of torture, in which they are confined to small pots and then twisted and contorted into grotesque shapes. To be sure, some bonsai give one this impression.

When properly done, however, the fantastic spirals and curves of a bonsai plant are solely the result of natural growth, aided by the craftsmanship of a competent bonsai artist.

Taming Wild Plants

Plants and other forms of vegetation are found everywhere in nature. Mountains, riverbanks, backyards, roadsides, and all kinds of nooks and crannies produce plant growth.

Plants are so abundant because they are endowed with an ability to adapt to their surroundings and the determination to survive.

If located in an arid area, plants sink their roots deep into the soil to seek water. If sunlight is scarce, they stretch their limbs up to access whatever light is available.

Bonsai, on the other hand, are cultivated and nurtured by artificial methods. Their environment is chosen for them, and they are compelled to adapt to it according to the wishes of the bonsai artist.

A bonsai artist selects a suitable plant or tree cutting, carefully transplants it into just the right kind of soil, and meticulously

bird-lime holly / exposed-root style /
height:8cm(3 inches) / rectangular vessel
Chinese wolfberry (Lycium chinensis)/
coiled-trunk / height:3.6cm(1.5 inches)/
small "thumb-sized" pot

waters, trims, fertilizes and otherwise cares for it. In this way, the plant is removed from its natural setting and protected from the elements.

As a result of such care, bonsai do not develop in the same way as do natural plants.

The amount of time it takes to grow a bonsai plant is directly proportional to its size. It may take up to 20 or 30 years for a large bonsai to attain perfection. There have been cases where a father and his sons are successively involved in the cultivation of a single bonsai plant. It is possible, however, to turn out a good small bonsai within a relatively short time. Despite their grandiose magnificence, large bonsai very often become fixed in shape and are not amenable to changes. Albeit lacking in large-scale grandeur, the poses of small bonsai plants can be recast without much trouble.

green maple / coiled-trunk / height:20cm
(8 inches) / round pot
fragrant maple / upright / height:14cm(5.5
inches) / rectangular pot

26

The growth of large bonsai plants is not easily threatened by the elements. Steadfastness is one of their salient qualities. On the other hand, small bonsai plants are frail, delicate and responsive to changes in the environment. Large bonsai plants are difficult to move around, and there is a limit to the places where they can be kept. Thanks to their small size, small bonsai plants can adorn desktops, windowsills, or be kept wherever deemed suitable. Small plants can be artistically employed to bring variation to our living spaces.

Chinese wolfberry / multi-trunk / height: 12cm(5 inches) / reddish-brown pot

This plant would be 30cm (12 inches) tall if straightened.

From left to right: Chinese elm shrub / multi-trunk/height:5cm(2 inches) clay pot
fragrant maple / cascade style / height:4cm(1.5 inches) / tall earthenware pot
Japanese red maple / semi-cascade style / width:13cm(5 inches) / shallow pot
azalea / multi-trunk / height:7cm(3 inches) /oval pot.

History

Schools

Bonsai was first conceived of and developed in China. Due to its huge size, China exhibits great regional variation in social customs and natural vegetation. As a result, different schools of bonsai cultivation have emerged.

The Lingnan, Ch'uan, Kiangsu, and Anhwei schools have had the greatest influence on modern bonsai cultivation.

Lingnan (Southern) School

Centered in the southern province of Kwangtung, this school of bonsai cultivation stresses the natural growth of bonsai plants, permitting only pruning with simple tools. Lingnan school bonsai plants are typically bold and unrestrained in both spirit and appearance. They retain an earthily natural quality even after years of cultivation. They require a relatively extended period of pruning to achieve success, however.

Since ancient times, Canton, the provincial capital of Kwangtung, has been a busy hub of business. During the Ch'ing Dynasty(1644-1911), the city witnessed frequent cultural exchanges with foreigners. The Lingnan school was exposed to the influence of other countries, Japan in particular, and Japanese bonsai styles began to rub off onto Lingnan bonsai. The Lingnan school and Japanese bonsai now share many stylistic similarities. Adherents of the Lingnan school often prefer locally available plants, such as "Cheuk Mui", Fukien tea, Chinese elm, and common jasmine orange trees, for their bonsai projects.

Ch'uan (Szechwan) School

Centered in Szechwan province, this school stresses upward spirals and twists. Each bonsai plant must have a focal point that is poetically referred to as a "pearl embraced by a cavorting dragon".

A potted plant painting by Ch'ing Dynasty (1644-1911) painter Chen Hsueh-hui, now part of the National Palace Museum's collection.

28

"Prosperity and Security," a painting by Ch'ing Dynasty painter Wu You-ju.

A poem on potted plants by a Ming Dynasty (1368-1644) poet.

程衡長李与竹刻善亦松小子
供繫簫樹小將遊生先諸園松
年十至幾植之樹一玩文盤盆
下天於聞樹盆刻竹之定嘉故
者之習多後

摘自明代王鳴韶秋定三家人傳

Szechwan is rich in natural flora. However, adherents of the Ch'uan school of bonsai largely confine themselves to the use of garden camelia, azalea, maiden-hair, "haitang", Chinese yew, and "snow-in-June."

Kiangsu School

The eastern coastal province of Kiangsu has been a center of cultural activity since ancient times. This school is divided into an eastern branch and a western branch.

The eastern branch is further divided into a Yang stream and a T'ung stream, and the western branch, into a Ch'angshou stream and a Soochow stream.

The Yang stream is characterized by its emphasis on twists and bends, so much so that even the tips of small sprigs of a bonsai plant, not to mention the main trunk, are preferably curled. The style is described as "one inch, three bends."

The T'ung stream also stresses twists and bends. The only difference between the T'ung and Yang streams is that the former calls for "two and a half bends." One distinctive feature of a T'ung bonsai plant is a trunk made up of three bends. The first two are near semi-circles a top a third, which has a lesser curvature.

Ch'angshou bonsai combine the special features of Ch'angshou, Nanking and Wushih bonsai styles. A Ch'angshou bonsai must meet the "six platforms, three bases, and one tip" requirement. Trunks are trained to attain six alternating bends, each referred to as a platform. The three main branches growing toward the rear are called the three bases. These accentuate the single tip at the top of the tree. The bark must be kept intact to achieve perfection.

Soochow has always been known for its exquisitely elaborate gardens. Soochow bonsai have developed into styles, referred to as "tree branches overhanging a cliff" and "wing-swept branches." A "wind-swept branches" bonsai is similar in form to the so-called "slanted-trunk" style. The former is distinguishable by a more obtuse angle of inclination, with overly extended branches protruding abruptly at the top. Pine trees are often used in this type of bonsai, and frequently are placed in living rooms because they resemble a beckoning gesture. As a result, they are informally known as "guest welcoming pines."

Anhwei School

Anhwei school bonsai are characterized by their screen-like horizontal extensions. At an early stage of cultivation, branches are trained sideways. Sometimes, several trees are combined by means of grafting to achieve a multi-dimensional geometric shape.

Origins

Bonsai has a long history in China and is said to owe its origin to the gardening arts of ancient times. According to historical records, gardening arts, such as "stone arranging," were practiced in the Shang Dynasty (1751-1111 B.C.).

During the Ch'in Dynasty, a large amount of forced manual labor was committed to the construction of palaces and imperial gardens. The 800 years between the Ch'in (221-207 B.C.) and Sui dynasties (581-618 A.D.) saw rapid progress in gardening techniques.

During the powerful and prosperous T'ang Dynasty (618-907 A.D.), greenery was no longer confined to traditional garden scenes, and people began to keep potted plants indoors as a visual delight.

The emergence of the art of bonsai during the T'ang Dynasty can be accounted for by two factors. First, growing prosperity in the cities denuded urban areas of green plants. As a result, a yearning for rural life began to take hold and plants were moved indoors to provide a measure of consolation.

Second, the severe winters of such cities as Ch'angan and Luoyang did not permit outdoor plant cultivation. Plants were therefore potted and kept indoors to provide a green touch.

In frescoes found in the mausoleum of Crown Prince Chang Huai, unearthed in 1971, two palace maids are portrayed holding potted plants. This is evidence that potted plants already held an important place in daily life during the T'ang Dynasty, more than a millennium ago.

Since the mid-T'ang era, bonsai has developed in two directions, "tree bonsai" and "rocky landscape bonsai." In the latter, the natural appearance of rocks figures prominently and plants are just a side attraction.

During the Sung Dynasty (960-1279 A.D.), intellectual pursuits, such as philosophical, religious, and artistic studies, were stressed at the expense of the country's military strength. Under such circumstances, bonsai developed greatly and became an established art.

The Yunlin Record of Rocks, an important early work on the art of bonsai, was published toward the end of the Northern Sung Dynasty (960-1127

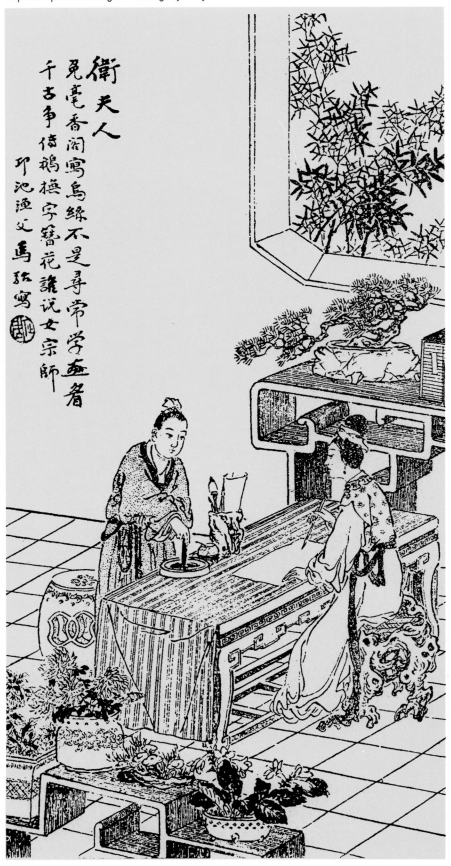

A woodblock print showing the popularity of potted plants during the Ch'ing Dynasty.

A.D.).

The book contained detailed descriptions of the types and properties of rocks found in all parts of the country. In addition, it explained how to choose pots and train trees.

During the Yuan Dynasty (1279-1368 A.D.), development of the arts came to a standstill and did not get back on course until the Ming Dynasty (1368-1644 A.D.). During the Ming Dynasty, numerous books and treatises were published on trees, garden scenes, the principles of flower and tree arranging, and how to find useful stones and rocks. Flower Mirror, by Hsu Hao-tzu, is worthy of special mention. In the book, bonsai techniques, training methods, species identification and other related factors are discussed in detail. During the Ming Dynasty, stands for presenting potted plants received as much attention as the visual artistry of the plants themselves.

Toward the end of the Ming Dynasty, because of advances in ceramic ware technology and improvements in glaze quality, colorful pots, many of which were objects of art in their own right, came into use.

During the reigns of the emperors K'anghsi, Yung-cheng and Ch'ien-lung, which spanned 130 years of the Ch'ing Dynasty (1644-1911 A.D.), new bonsai styles that stressed elegance were developed. Many members of the literati took delight in growing trees that were said to be compatible with their social standing. During this period,

A Ming Dynasty woodblock print showing a potted plant.

the most sought-after pots were fine clay pots from Yihsin Kiln in Chingteh Town, Kiangsi Province.

During the Ch'ing Dynasty, many books were published on bonsai. The most interesting volume is a book by Chen Fu-yau, who discusses such topics as how to select and train trees and how to grow them under different conditions in various parts of the country. Some modern botanical concepts are found in this work. Chen's book was later introduced to Japan, where it had a significant influence on Japanese bonsai styles.

The country's strength and fortunes rapidly declined toward the end of the Ch'ing Dynasty and its ports were forced open by foreign powers.

Foreign businessmen, backed by military power, began making inroads into the Chinese market. Japanese flower shops mushroomed in big cities, like Shanghai and Tientsin. At the time, the country was beset with political unrest and widespread poverty, and the Chinese were simply too preoccupied with their lot to cultivate bonsai.

In the early years of the Republic, the nation was prevented by frequent civil wars from accomplishing much in the way of bonsai art, and many valuable works were destroyed.

During the last 20 years, bonsai has become fashionable again as a result of the country's social stability and rapid economic growth.

A painting by Chin Ting-piao, a Ch'ing Dynasty artist.

31

Bonsai plants must be properly cared for in order to maintain balanced growth.

Key Factors for the Cultivation of Bonsai

Sunlight

In a natural environment, plants derive nourishment from nutrients absorbed from the soil through their roots. They also depend on sunlight for survival, as it stimulates the process of photosynthesis whereby plants manufacture their own source of energy. Photosynthesis is an innate activity and cannot be halted. Therefore it is important to keep each plant exposed to an appropriate amount of sunlight, otherwise its growth and development will be adversely affected.

Plants suffering from under-exposure to sunlight will compensate by developing larger leaves to absorb what light is available. In the long-run, these plants will become thin and feeble, eventually withering and dying.

Both lamplight and sunlight induce photosynthesis. Ultraviolet rays necessary to the healthy growth of plants are not present in lamplight, however. Sunlight, therefore, is the only adequate source of energy for plants. Kept in a poorly lit place, most plants will die.

Over-exposure to sunlight can also be harmful. Plants with very thin leaves can be burned by too much exposure to direct sunlight. When shallow pots are used to house bonsai, care must be taken to ensure that the rays of the sun do not dehydrate the soil and deprive the plant of the water it so desperately needs. In general, the physical characteristics of a plant, as well as the size

32

Taiwan trident maple / upright / root-over-rock / height:15cm(3 inches)/ shallow rectangular pot

of the pot it is housed in, will determine the optimal duration and intensity of its exposure to the sun.

Plants are generally phototactive, meaning that they tend to grow toward the source of light. Under normal lighting conditions, a bonsai plant should be repositioned every few days to keep its growth balanced. If a bonsai plant kept near a window remains in the same position for many days in a row, its leaves will come to face the window, and the so-called "frontal" view of the bonsai plant will become its "rear." Therefore, bonsai plants must be repositioned every now and then in relation to the source of light.

Water

Watering is a common problem for bonsai enthusiasts. The question of how much and how often to water is not easily answered. If one waters not enough, the plant will die of thirst. If one waters too much, bacteria may multiply and the roots of the plant may rot.

A basic rule of thumb is to first sprinkle a small amount of water over the soil of a plant and wait until the moisture is totally absorbed. Then continue to sprinkle water on until the soil is well-moistened.

In the spring, plants develop buds and sprouts. Providing sufficient water is especially important during this season of growth. Overwatering, however, will result in excessive growth and distancing between branch nodes. In order to avoid these problems, water each plant once every day, moistening the soil thoroughly. When the weather is overcast or rainy, reduce the amount of water used or water at longer intervals.

In the summer, plants need more water as hot weather dries soil quickly. Water once in the morning and once in the evening. The soil of young, delicate plants should be kept moistened at all times to prevent it from drying up.

In the fall, plants build up reserves of nutrients to prepare for the winter. As the weather becomes colder and damper, reduce the amount of water supplied to your bonsai.

During the winter, deciduous trees enter a state of dormancy and the growth of evergreen trees slows considerably. As a result, both types of trees require very little water, just enough to keep the soil they are planted in slightly moist.

Watering is not a rigidly inflexible procedure, but must be done in accordance with the density of leaves and branches. All plants can, to a certain degree, tolerate and adapt to hostile living environments. For example, prolonged exposure to a high degree of humidity can induce the development of humidity-resistant characteristics in a plant and cause the retardation of its drought-resistant abilities. On the other hand, given time, plants also can adapt to arid conditions. It must be pointed out that slightly excessive watering is preferrable to inadequate watering. Inexperienced non-professional cultivators of bonsai plants should bear this in mind if their busy schedules prevent them from spending time with their plants. Dehydration can cause irreparable damage to plants. On the other hand, a plant grown in highly humid conditions can hold out for

Occasionally cultivators will place their plant in an unsuitably damp and dim environment, while continuing to water it the usual amount. When placed in a dim and damp environment, the evaporation of excess water is slowed and the plant becomes water-logged. The remedy is simple - move the plant to a more sunlit environment.

33

For convenience, many bonsai artists place their plants on a large table and water them all at once.

considerable time. If cultivators make timely efforts to remedy the situation, deaths can be avoided.

There have also been cases in which bonsai plants suffered because they were placed in hardened sticky soil. In such cases, watering is to no avail because water is drained away through the gap between the inner surface of the pot and the hardened block of soil. As a result, plants are denied an adequate amount of water. There are also people who pack soil too tightly, so that water cannot permeate the soil completely and much of it is lost through evaporation. Under such circumstances, plants wither and die.

There is a correct and an incorrect way to sprinkle water on a plant. The correct way is to sprinkle the water around the upper rim of the pot containing the plant, so that the water seeps down through the soil until it reaches the roots. Excess water is drained away through holes in the bottom of the pot. A pot with several small holes in the bottom is the best kind for bonsai plants. Sprinkle water evenly and gently, without causing the topsoil to become uneven.

Do not place a plant directly under the scorching sun when watering it. A bead of water on the surface of a leaf has an effect similar to that of a magnifying glass when it is used to reflect the sun's rays onto an object. The leaf will burn.

Some cultivators of bonsai have a habit of keeping their bonsai plants in trays filled with water, thinking that this will guarantee an uninterrupted supply of water for the plants. This actually does no good, except for a few species of plants which absorb copious amounts of water. When arranging bonsai plants, do so in accordance with their capacity for absorbing water. This will make the task of watering much easier.

Soil

Soil provides water and nutrients to whatever vegetation grows in it. It is indispensable to the development of a plant.

Good drainage and the ability to conserve water, two apparently mutually exclusive characteristics, are what one should look for in soil. "Granular soil" with grains that are not readily soluble is generally acceptable. Every grain of soil should be absorbent and there should be enough room between grains to allow the passage of excess water. Both good drainage and the ability to conserve water are found in soil made up of such "grains." In addition, ventilation is excellent in granular soil and roots can easily develop in it. So it is ideal for plant growth.

Granular soil can be bought from vendors, or, bonsai enthusiasts can prepare their own in the following manner. First, choose soil that will not dissolve or turn into paste in water. After watering the soil, dry and harden it by leaving it in the sun for three days. Eliminate impurities and separate grains of different sizes by using different sieves. During the drying process, germs and bacteria are killed by ultra-violet rays. This will save a lot of trouble in the future.

If circumstances do not permit drying in the sun, one can "bake" the soil in a flat metal pan at a temperature of up to 200 degrees Celsius (400°F). Heat slowly. Stir and churn constantly to keep the soil from being burned. Sift after the soil has become completely dry and has cooled down. Germs and bacteria are killed in the heating process.

Some people are partial to so-called "black soil," "farmland soil," and "vegetable garden soil," which are said to be exceptionally fertile. These types of soil are often not very balanced in nutrient content. For example, soil excavated from farmland may be rich in nitrogen but deficient in phosphorus. Plants grown in such soil are either leafy but flowerless, or produce a few flowers but do not bear fruit. Because of this, soil devoid of impurities is preferred although it might be less fertile. Fertilizer will be applied to it later according to the needs of the plants grown in it.

Weather

In the spring, after waking up from a prolonged dormancy, plants begin to develop

When watering, it is necessary to make sure water reaches the inner surface and bottom of the pot.

Harmful bacteria is killed by the sun's rays.

sprouts. So they need a lot of water during this period of the year. If they are given too much water, however, excessive growth will result and the distribution of leaves will become uneven. As a result, the plant's appearance will be ruined. In the spring, in spite of the warm weather, sporadic cold fronts can still wreak havoc. When a cold front arrives, keep bonsai plants warm and move them to places where they can enjoy maximum exposure to the sun.

During the summer, plants grow at a

Sieves for sifting.

Soil with grains of different sizes.

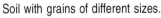

Sift soil in order to eliminate powdery dirt, which impedes drainage.

A rare Taiwan pieris plant with a height of 21cm (8 inches) in a square vessel, photographed in June (1) and November (2) and during the flowering season in spring (3).

1

3

2

rapid pace and must be supplied with an adequate amount of nutrients and water. Summer is also a time when the eggs of harmful insects hatch and many types of diseases spread. Both pests and diseases must be stopped before they cause major problems.

In the fall, plants appear to stop growing, but in reality a fascinating array of activities continue to take place. Plants voraciously absorb nutrients in order to build up reserves for the coming winter months. After storing enough energy-producing materials, the chlorophyll in the leaves of a plant is replaced with carotene. As a result, the leaves change color, first from green to yellow, and then from yellow to a breathtaking red. If not supplied with sufficient amounts of fertilizer, plants will continue to produce their own nutrients through photosynthesis. As a result, the chlorophyll in their leaves will remain undisplaced by carotene, and the leaves will not change color. In the event that a plant fails to absorb an adequate amount of

nutrients before the onset of winter, it will die.

As the growth of some plants comes to a complete standstill during the winter season, it is advisable to give them less water and fertilizer while the weather remains cold and damp. In addition, avoid pruning during the winter months because cuts and wounds will heal very slowly.

Fertilizer

Plants cannot survive if they are denied an adequate amount of life-sustaining nutrients. In the wilderness, plants absorb nutrients from soil through their well developed root systems. Plants confined to pots are a different story. It is necessary to replenish the nutrient supply of the soil in which plants are grown as soon as it becomes depleted. Plant growth is powered by such elements as potassium, iron, copper, zinc, magnesium molybdenum, manganese, calcium, oxygen, hydrogen, nitrogen, phosphorus, sulfur, boron, and carbon. Of these, nitrogen, phosphorus, and potassium are the three most important elements for balanced plant growth and must be periodically added to the soil in which plants grow. The others are elements normally found in ordinary soil.

Nitrogenous fertilizers are commonly referred to as "leaf fertilizers" because they make leaves strong and luxuriant. Phosphate fertilizers, known as "flower fertilizers," fatten flower buds and cause flowers to bloom radiantly. Potash fertilizers are called "root fertilizers" because they nourish roots and help plants to develop strong trunks, branches and root systems. Growers can mix their own blends of fertilizer.

Fertilizers from natural sources are called organic fertilizers, and include oil cakes, fish meal, bone meal, and animal dung. Generally speaking, organic fertilizers made up of animal tissues are phosphate fertilizers and organic fertilizers made up of plant tissues are rich in nitrogen. Organic fertilizers are mild in nature and their effects are more gradual and longer lasting. Therefore, they do not cause problems with overdosing and are suitable for bonsai plants. Unfortunately, their odor attracts ants, cockroaches, and other insects.

Inorganic fertilizers are manufactured at fertilizer plants. Devoid of impurities, they are highly potent, highly efficacious, and easy to use. Be careful when using them, however, as they are capable of inflicting serious harm on plants if used excessively.

Inorganic fertilizers normally come with user's guides and small spoons. Before using, one should first read the guides and apply the fertilizer in strict accordance with the enclosed instructions. In user's guides the percentage ratio of the fertilizer's nitrogen content, phosphorus content, and potassium content are listed in fixed order (for example 10-20-30). In this case, 10-20-30 means the fertilizer is 10 percent nitrogen, 20 percent phosphorus, and 30 percent potassium. To dilute, dissolve each gram of the chemical fertilizer in 1 liter of water.

Of course, to meet the particular needs of each plant, a grower can mix his own fertilizer with homogenous single element fertilizers. In the event of excessive application, the grower should remove the fertilizer on the topsoil and immerse the entire plant in fresh water to reduce the concentration of fertilizer and to reduce damage to the plant.

Fertilizer in a granular or small-slab form works more slowly than fertilizer in a liquid or powder form. When growing bonsai plants, slow-effect fertilizers are preferred. By applying slow-effect fertilizers, a grower can control exactly the growth of his or her plants.

Diseases and Insects

Plant diseases and pests are, in most cases a result of the mismanagement of water, soil, and the environment. The best way to prevent plant diseases and pests is to give plants an appropriate amount of water, use "clean" soil, keep the areas surrounding bonsai plants clean, and apply preventative antiseptics at regular intervals.

Plant Diseases

Root rot - Root rot is the most commonly occuring bonsai plant disease. It is caused by soil contamination, water logging, and over-application of fertilizer. A bonsai plant which has contracted root rot should be immediately uprooted. The soil must be dumped and replaced with new soil and the pot should be thoroughly washed. Diseased roots should be cut off and damaged branches and leaves, trimmed.

Red mildew - Red mildew is commonly found in the rose family in the muggy, humid months of April and May. Reddish brown spots first appear on the surface of the foliage. These spots will grow and harden into tiny nuggets. Further deterioration will retard or obstruct growth and lead to a premature death. If affected plants are not immediately isolated, the cysts released from them can spread the disease to other plants. To cure affected plants, it is necessary to spray them with a fungicide once every week for three to four weeks.

Powdery mildew - Powdery mildew is most commonly found among plants kept in poorly lit, humid and relatively cool areas. Deciduous trees, such as maple and elm, contract this disease easily. One of its symptoms is that fiber-like mildew develops on the surface of new leaves of affected trees in spring and disappears in summer as temperatures rise. When treating affected trees, it is necessary to clip the affected leaves and spray the plants with a Dithane solution before moving them to a well-lit and well-ventilated place. The incidence of this disease can be reduced by sprinkling a lime-and-sulfur solution onto trees after they have shed their leaves.

Pinequiver - Pinequiver is most commonly found among coniferous trees in the summer. A typical symptom is that brownish spots develop on the surface of leaves.

In its initial stage, the disease does not have a very serious effect on plants and is frequently overlooked by growers. However, the condition of affected trees will deteriorate rapidly if the disease goes untreated. Leaves will turn brown and fall off and the branches of the affected plants will wither. Therefore, it is important to deal with the problem at an early stage, by spraying a Bordeaux mixture on them.

A green maple afflicted with white mildew.

A shrub althea, plagued with leaf rollers. The curled leaves are a symptom.

Insects

Insects can cause even greater harm to small bonsai plants than diseases. Therefore, it is necessary to pay close attention to prevention. While watering growers should look carefully for insect bites on leaves and branches and insect excrement about the plants. If the insects discovered are large in size or few in number, they can be picked off with forceps. If the insects are small in size or numerous, it will be necessary to spray insecticide on both the top and bottom of each leaf. Insects protected by slick exo-skeletons can be quite impervious to insecticide. They can be dealt with effectively if a sticky dispersant is added to the insecticide, however.

Harm done to plants by aphids and scale insects is difficult to detect because they leave only sucking marks, not bites. They are most active in the spring and summer and special care must be taken to prevent them from causing trouble.

Aphids are even more difficult to detect on the surface of young branches because of their protective coloration. Scale insects look like abalone and can be brushed off with tooth brushes. Both types of pests can be eliminated by spraying Sumithion on plants.

Styles

Bonsai, like fashion, is a style oriented art form. The most popular bonsai styles are the following: single-trunk, twin-trunk, multi-trunk, cascade, literati, clinging-to-rock, root-over-rock, raft, exposed-root, and landscape (group planting or forest).

1. Single-Trunk:

A bonsai in this style has only a single trunk. Because of its simplicity, it is difficult to be creative with a single-trunk bonsai. Various sub-styles have arisen from single-trunk, including upright-trunk, coiled-trunk, slanting-trunk, and broom. The upright-trunk is the most common. A bonsai of the coiled-trunk style features a trunk that is coiled in an elegant manner, with its apex directly above its base. A slanting-trunk bonsai leans to one side. If such a bonsai has a nicely curved trunk, it will be very attractive to the eye. A broom bonsai displays upward curving branches that resemble the upside-down bristles of a broom.

2. Twin-trunk and Tri-trunk:

A bonsai in this style features two or three trunks that contrast with one another in some way. Twin-trunk and tri-trunk bonsai are usually the result of grafting or cutting.

3. Multi-trunk:

This style of bonsai features more than three trunks. Each trunk should be of a different shape and size, but when taken together, they should all complement one another.

4. Literati:

A literati style bonsai displays an elegance similar to that of a traditional Chinese scholar. Such bonsai should always be tall and slender.

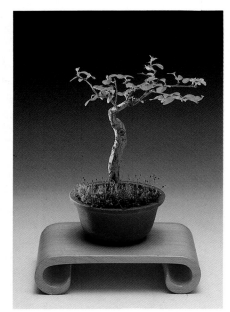

crape myrtle / twisted-trunk / height: 9cm(3.5 inches) / black unglazed pot

40

Chinese elm / multi-trunk / height: 18cm(6 inches) / shallow round pot

This bonsai was created through layering. The mother tree was 60cm (24 inches) in height. Layering preserves the appearance of the mother tree, and makes potting and repotting an easy job.

taiwania / tri-trunk / height:12cm(5 inches) / shallow oval pot

This bonsai was created through cutting. Taiwania roots grow rapidly, so planting them in a shallow container is troublesome, re-potting is required every 6 months and it takes three years to cultivate a bonsai like this.

crape myrtle / twin-trunk / height:11cm(4.5 inches) / square pot

This bonsai originally consisted of two separate plants, but after several years their roots joined together.

5. Cascade:

In this style, the trunk and branches of the tree grow downward like those of plants which grow on precipitous mountains and steep cliffs. If the branches reach below the level of the bottom of the pot, the bonsai is called a full cascade, and if not, then it is called a semi-cascade.

Japanese red maple / slanting/ horizontal length:20cm(8 inches)/ tripod-bottomed round pot

This bonsai was created by grafting together two cuttings from different Japanese maple species.

star jasmine / cascade / vertical length: 7cm(3 inches) / tall square pot

Creepers have a natural cascade style, but because their roots and branches are soft, one should fix them in place with rope for the first two months after potting.

trident maple / semi-cascade/ horizontal length:18cm(7 inches)/ tripod-bottomed round pot

A product of side grafting.

6. Raft:

Bonsai in this style are formed by lying a trunk flat on its side, covering it with earth, and allowing branches to emerge and grow in a straight line. To create a successful raft style bonsai, one must trim off all branches on three sides of the trunk, and lay the trunk down with the remaining branches extending upward. When covered with soil, this bonsai will come to resemble several small bonsai growing in a row.

Japanese serissa / raft / height:10cm(4 inches) / shallow oval pot

Japanese serissa is an ideal species for the raft style. Just lay the trunk flat on the ground and remove excess downward branches. Then cover with soil and allow the branches that protrude to grow upward.

shrub althea / cascade / vertical length: 24cm(10 inches) / round pot inset in rock

To cultivate a bonsai in cascade style, one should choose plants with slanting trunks or with an innate tendency for horizontal growth.

43

A natural clinging-to-rock tree.

green maple / slanting and root-over-rock / height:20cm (8 inches) / yellow unglazed pot

The ratio between the sizes of rock and tree can be extremely varied in the clinging-to-rock/root-over-rock style.

(left) sliver maple / root-over-rock / rock height:6cm(2.5 inches) / yellow oblong unglazed pot
(right) Chinese elm / root-over-rock / rock height:5cm(2 inches) / blue square pot

7. Root-over-rock, Clinging-to-rock:

A root-over-rock style bonsai features exposed roots which cling to a rock below them, leaving a small space between the rock and the point where the roots attach to the main trunk.

A clinging-to-rock style bonsai is planted in the crevices or holes of a rock, which then serves as a pot for the plant. If the rock is well-balanced, there is no need to add pots or other supporting items.

8. Exposed-root:

The roots of any plant are compelled to adapt to various differences in geological structure and environmental conditions. As a result, they display complicated and fascinating patterns. A bonsai in the exposed root style is created for the expressed purpose of revealing the beauty of its roots. Roots are either totally or partially exposed.

9. Shari (peeled trunk):

    This style features bonsai stripped of leaves and bark. A difficult style to achieve because of the danger of killing the bonsai material, only experienced cultivators should attempt a shari bonsai.

10. Landscape (group planting or forest):

    This style is free and open. One can plant from three to three hundred small bonsai in a single container. The objective is to create a landscape or forest scene. Sometimes tiny houses, bridges and figures are added to a landscape bonsai.

Shrub althea / shari / height:32cm(13 inches) / yellow unglazed pot

Japanese gray-bark elm / group planting / height (the tallest tree): 20cm(8 inches) / shallow oval pot

    In group planting style, the upright growing trees are used to form the main body of the forest and the twisted-trunk trees are used to vary the scene.

Japanese premna / shari / height:35cm (14 inches) / black unglazed pot

    A bonsai in shari style should be simple, unique, and powerful.

All the trees seen in this picture were cultivated from fruit seeds; from left to right: persimmon, orange, grape; years of cultivation: 4,5,6

Cultivation

Using fruit seeds is the easiest way to grow your own bonsai from scratch.
left: longan / right: lemon

Sowing Seeds

Great pleasure can be derived from watching a seed gradually evolve from a seedling into a young plant, and then, after several years, into a mature bonsai. This process can take as long as several decades, however. Only very patient and very skilled bonsai artists are able to turn out a bonsai that lives up to their expectations by starting from a seed.

Seeds can be obtained from plants or bought from vendors. When buying seeds, care must be taken to ensure that they are fresh. Seeds bought from vendors preferably should be kept in the freezer of a refrigerator. A short "hibernation" is beneficial to their germination.

Fruit is also a convenient source of seeds and fruit seeds germinate easily. Fruit seeds should be sown immediately after they are cleaned of any remaining fruit tissue. In the event that they have to be stored until the arrival of suitable season, seeds can be "preserved" by the following method: Place a layer of small stones at the bottom of an unglazed basin and follow with alternate layers of seeds and sand. After this is done, keep the whole thing in a well-ventilated place.

Seeds are preferably sown in the spring and fall. March is the most suitable time because the mild weather during this month is conducive to plant growth. If seeds are sown in the fall, the severe weather during the coming winter can have an adverse effect upon the growth of the emerging seedlings.

On the day before seeds are sown, they should be soaked in water for 24 hours. After absorbing water, mature seeds will sink to the bottom, and undesirable seeds will remain afloat.

While seeds can germinate in many types of pots, shallow unglazed pots are best. Before sowing seeds, wash the pot thoroughly to forestall the incidence of plant disease and to prevent insects from causing trouble. Next place a piece of mesh at the bottom of the pot, followed by a layer of coarse-grained soil. Then fill the pot 80 percent full with medium-grained soil. Seeds are now evenly arranged atop the soil before being covered with a layer of fine-grained soil. This layer of soil should be just thick enough to cover the seeds. The pot is then placed in water to absorb moisture.

Before the seeds germinate, it is necessary to keep the soil appropriately moist. Sprinkling should be done with utmost care to prevent the formation of pockmarks on the surface of the soil. The pots containing the seeds should be kept in well-ventilated and well-lit places. In the event that such an arrangement still cannot ensure a warm

Scions mass produced for bonsai cultivation are grown in seedbeds.

enough temperature, the pots can each be covered with glass to produce a "greenhouse" effect. The glass also serves to prevent evaporation and keeps birds from pecking at the seeds.

Depending on its type, it takes a seed 10 days to two months to germinate. After germination, cotyledons will appear, followed by full-fledged leaves. After the cotyledons fall off, the cultivator should churn the soil along the inner surface of the vessel housing the plant to make the soil less tightly packed. By this time, most plants will have developed spiraling roots.

Therefore, it is also necessary to "loosen" the soil from the bottom up and to cut off one-third of the main roots. In this way, one can foster the healthy growth of roots and improve the appearance of the trunk base.

After one-third of their roots are cut off, plants can be transplanted into small pots. One month after transplanting, the cultivator can apply a small amount of fertilizer. One year later, the plants become seedlings and are ready to be transformed into small, medium, or large bonsai plants.

① ② ③ ④

⑤ ⑥

Growing plants from seeds, procedures.

All the plants housed in this vessel were cultivated from cuttings.

Cutting

Planting and cultivating a piece of a branch cut from a parent plant is a common method of producing bonsai. Bonsai grown from cuttings are similar to their parent plants both in appearance and growth pattern. As this method is much quicker and simpler than cultivating a plant from a seed, it is popular among bonsai artists.

The best time to take a cutting is in the humid summer season. When taking a cutting from a deciduous tree, plant it only after new leaves have begun to bloom on its parent.

Cutting method: Cut a healthy branch or twig from a parent plant and trim to a length of about five or six inches, with a maximum of four to five leaves. Remove any leaves or debris from the lower portion, as it will be planted in the soil and any remaining leaves will decay and cause bacteria problems. Make sure that the bottom is unblemished. If the cutting is from a type of plant that does not easily develop roots, split its bottom slightly and insert a pebble into the split. This will help it to absorb water and nutrients.

Some plants display marks on their branches, indicating spots where roots can develop. When taking a cutting from a parent plant, make your cut just below such marks so that they end up at the bottom of the cutting. Soak the cutting in water for 24 hours.

One can enable the cutting to develop roots more quickly by applying an appropriate amount of root growth stimulant.

This stimulant is available in both liquid and powder forms. Root growth stimulant in the liquid form should be diluted with water before use. After diluting the stimulant with water, place the cutting in an upright position in a bowl of the liquid for several hours before planting. If using the powdered root growth stimulant, take care to not dampen it, as this will greatly reduce its effectiveness. When using the powdered stimulant, thoroughly coat the bottom section of the cutting with powder placed in a dry, shallow basin.

Cutting procedures.

Before developing roots, a cutting relies mainly upon its own meager nutrient reserves and starch production for survival. It will develop roots as a matter of course after it begins to run low on nutrients and is forced to seek additional sources of sustenance. Do not rashly add fertilizer to a cutting, or its roots might not develop normally.

When planting a cutting, use a shallow basin because it will facilitate the growth of a more balanced root network. Do not pack the soil too tightly, or it might block the development of roots. If planting more than one cutting in a single vessel, plant the shorter ones near the rim and the taller ones near the center so that all the cuttings receive an adequate amount of sunlight and ventilation. Also, when planting several cuttings together, arrange them so that their branches touch one another. This will help to prevent dehydration and will keep them more firmly planted.

Cuttings from coniferous trees take a long time to develop roots. As for cuttings from other kinds of trees, as soon as roots emerge through the holes at the bottom of the pot, about three to four months after planting, the cuttings should be immediately transplanted, otherwise roots from separate cuttings will become entangled with each

other, making transplanting difficult.

Cuttings can be planted either vertically or horizontally in soil. Techniques aimed at producing such special effects as double-trunks, triple-trunks, and so on are also possible. By choosing branches and twigs with a special appearance to take as cuttings, one will save a lot of time with regard to training in the future.

Hardened or tightly packed soil should be loosened and have holes punched into it before cuttings are inserted in order to keep the cuttings undamaged. When taking cuttings from parent plants that produce flowers of different colors, choose branches and twigs with flowers of different colors to ensure that the bonsai cultivated from them will also produce more than one color of flower.

Layering

Layering refers to a special propagation method whereby parts of a plant are made to develop their own roots before being removed from the parent plant. Layering methods include bend layering (also called earth layering) or air layering. Bend layering is achieved by bending branches close to the ground, then covering their tips with soil, and keeping them in this position until they develop roots. Air layering, however, is the more commonly used layering method.

Cutting and layering are the two most efficient methods to obtain scions which retain the outward appearance of their parent plants. Layering also has the additional advantage of being appearance-preserving.

The best time of the year for layering is when spring changes into summer, because this is the time when buds sprout. Summer heat also can help increase survival rates.

The following is an outline of air layering procedures:

1. Choose healthy, pest-free parent plants.

(Apply fertilizer preferably one or two months before layering.)

2. Prepare some coarse, medium and fine-grained granular soil and keep a black plastic pot, metal wire, a pair of scissors, and a grafting knife handy.

3. Trim leaves to reduce the weight of target scions.

4. Select a point beneath which roots are expected to grow, and use the grafting knife to "ring" the target branch, cutting into the xylem.

5. "Ring" the branch at another point below the first cut. The distance between the two points should be 1.5 to 2 times the diameter of the branch.

6. Remove the bark completely to expose the xylem. Otherwise, the exposed part may easily heal over.

7. Cut open a black plastic pot (a black plastic pot is chosen because it absorbs heat readily and heat stimulates the development of roots) from the rim all the way down to the hole at its bottom.

8. Pull the branch through the hole at the bottom of the black plastic pot. The hole should have a diameter equal to that of the branch it surrounds. Close the cut edges of the pot back together using a piece of steel wire.

9. Pour coarse, medium and fine-grained soil into the pot, in that order (the bottom of the pot is preferably covered by layers of waterweed to prevent the loss of soil and moisture), and anchor the pot of soil to the branch using a piece of wire. Sprinkle with water until water drips from the bottom of the pot.

10. Water frequently to keep the soil moistened. Two or three months later, roots will develop. As roots emerge from the cut and other cracks, dismantle the black plastic pot and remove the soil to expose the barked part of the branch.

11. Remove the branch from the parent plant.

12. Trim the roots and prepare the scion for

transplant. (For transplanting procedures, see page 68.)

Moist sphagnum moss also can be used in layering. After barking according to the procedures described above, wrap slightly moistened sphagnum moss around the ringed part of the branch. The size of the layers of sphagnum moss, when wrapped with polyethylene sheeting, should be about two or three times the diameter of the branch. Use wire to fasten the layers of sphagnum moss around the branch to hold it in place. The layers of sphagnum moss must not be fastened too tightly, nor too loosely.

Following this, the sphagnum moss must be kept moistened and the scion should be exposed to an abundant amount of sunlight. After whitish roots emerge, the branch can be cut off from the parent plant and the polyethylene sheeting can be removed. At this time, the new roots are still frail and vulnerable and easily broken. So, the sphagnum moss must not be removed when the branch is cut from the parent plant (or the stool, as it is commonly called). It should be potted along with the branch.

The sphagnum moss can be removed a year later, when the scion's root system becomes well developed. After removing the sphagnum moss, an effort must be made to sort out the roots before the scion is transplanted into another vessel.

As for rare species of plants, or slow growing plants that do not easily lend themselves to layering, it is necessary to tighten a piece of metallic wire at selected points on their branches. In this way, the branches will become swollen at these points because of the restricted passage of nutrients. One can then remove the wire and the bark at these points.

Layering procedures.

Grafting

The purpose of grafting is to combine scions from precious species to "stocks" of the same species in order to produce new plants. In grafting, the firm foundation provided by a stock is combined with the beautiful shape of a scion to produce an offspring with the best characteristics of each. An additional advantage of the method is that it can help the bonsai artist obtain scions that are normally difficult to cultivate. Grafting is possible only between closely related species of plants. Young plants derived from grafting are more healthy and blossom and bear fruit earlier than those grown from seeds. Grafting is quite a difficult method requiring skillful hands for its successful application. If skillfully applied however, this method can increase survival rates.

Stocks can be prepared by such methods as cleft grafting, splice grafting, bud grafting and "belly" grafting. Of these, cleft crafting and "belly" grafting are the more commonly used methods.

Cleft Grafting : In this form of grafting, a stock is first prepared by cutting all the upper parts off of a plant, leaving a flat-topped trunk. Make sure that the cut is

Both the bonsai plant and the stub pictured here are from the same parent plant, a Japanese gray-bark elm.

The stub develops into a new plant within a year.

Both layering and grafting were applied in the creation of this bonsai plant.

Layering ensures a high survival rate, but can leave scars on the bark.

Layering ensures a high survival rate, but can leave scars on the bark.

level (parallel to the ground), and is smooth. Next, make a vertical wedge-shaped incision into the xylem of the stock. Prepare the scion to be grafted onto the stock by making two cuts at its bottom so that it tapers to a point. Then, fit the tapering end of the scion into the vertical wedge-shaped cut on the stock. The scion should fit into the wedge-shaped cut perfectly, but part of the "wounds" (where the bark of the scion has been exposed as a result of being cut into a point) should extend above the incision. Wrap string around the stock and scion to hold them together.

Cleft grafting is best performed in the spring before plants begin to bud. Remember to remove the string after the wounds on the graft heal.

Belly grafting : Belly grafting is similar to cleft grafting except that the scion is inserted into the stock so that it sticks directly out from the trunk at an angle perpendicular to the ground. To prevent the scion from falling out of the stock, it must be held in place by a wrapping of several layers of sphagnum

Wounds bound with elastic bands heal quickly.

Cut off the branches below and remove the string after the wounds have healed.

moss. When the scion and the trunk grow together, the moss can be removed.

Roots can also benefit from the process of grafting. The roots of each plant have a special pattern of their own. If one has two plants of the same species, one of which has fascinating roots and the other an attractive branch network, they can be grafted together to make a new plant with the best characteristics of both. To do so, cut the plant with the attractive roots at a point just above the root area. Take the plant with the desired branches, make a cut in a spot just above its roots, and bind the wounds of the two plants together. Then place them both in a single pot. After the wounds heal completely, sever the two joined plants at a point just below where the wounds used to be. The original plant should now produce an attractive branch network.

The main purpose of grafting is to improve the appearance of a plant. Needless to say, the first year following the grafting is a time of great uncertainty as to whether or not the plant will survive. One must pay close attention to the new tree, encouraging its rapid growth and the development of new leaves and branches. In addition, be sure to erect props next to the new plant so that it remains fixed in place and doesn't fall over.

Japanese red maple / slanting / height: 21cm(8 inches) / circular shallow vessel

Separation (Division)

Some species of plants produce creeping tendrils from their roots or trunks, and if separated from the parent plant, such tendrils can often grow into a healthy plant. Separation is a method of propagating bonsai by severing these tendrils from parent plants. This method is commonly applied to plant species which germinate easily.

The best time to carry out separation is during re-potting, especially during the spring when plants enjoy a growth surge.

The process is as follows: uproot a parent plant and remove the soil from its root system. Find the tendril and cut it from the root system. Pot both the parent plant and the tendril.

Sometimes plants are split in half along their axis and the two halves are re-potted. If placed side by side in a pot, they create an unusual visual treat.

The main purpose of separation is to improve the appearance of a plant. By means of separation, one can highlight the special features of a plant whose overall appearance is not very pleasing. The deliberate splitting of plants into two or more separate parts is

unnatural, however, and involves technical problems. Therefore, plants obtained by separation often do not survive. This method should not be too frequently or rashly adopted.

When separating a plant, it is necessary to first take a close look at its texture. If a cut is made way off the axis, one of the resulting plants could have too much xylem, while the other nothing but bark.

After splitting, an adequate amount of sulfur mixture or sealant should be applied to the wounds to forestall decay. The wounds should be covered with sphagnum moss to replenish moisture supply.

Plants thus obtained are usually not firmly rooted, but can be held in place by being anchored to props. As separation inevitably affects the growth of plants, it takes time for them to resume healthy growth. Therefore, they should not be trimmed and trained until new roots emerge.

When the two plants are placed together it becomes obvious that they are from the same parent plant.

53

A banyan tree.

Collecting from Mountains

Exposed to intense sunlight, strong wind, insects and animals, plants growing in mountain areas often display a natural, distinctive grace and flair for survival that makes them ideal for bonsai cultivation. This is especially true of those plants which thrust their way through rocks or grow from cracks overhanging inaccessible abysses.

Before collecting plants from mountains, one should first have a commitment to environmental conservation. Wild plants growing in nature are a precious treasure that must be properly protected.

There are, indeed, selfish bonsai growers or sellers who ruthlessly dig up whatever they run into so long as it fits their purposes. It must be stressed that plants not properly prepared usually do not survive. More often than not, arbitrary digging leads to depletion of natural resources. Therefore, the collection of plants from nature must be based on careful consideration and the principle that ecology and the beauty of nature are not to be violated.

Plants are best collected during drizzles, especially in the spring before plants germinate. As for evergreen plants, the best time for collection is during the so-called "plum-rain" period of the year. A "collector" should bring a spade, a hoe, containers, a pruning hook,

Most stubs for sale are collected from the outdoors.

and an ample amount of sphagnum moss.

Plants growing in rock cracks can be removed if they can be readily dug out. In the event a certain plant cannot be removed without the application of much force, however, it is better that it is left alone. If it is forcibly uprooted, its branches and roots will be damaged. Seedlings that emerge from seeds that fall from trees or bushes can be removed without doing much damage to the environment.

When digging up a plant, care must be taken to avoid damaging its roots. Tips of roots, if they cannot be removed unscathed, should be clipped. After being removed, the roots and part of the trunk of the target plant should be wrapped with sphagnum moss. Unnecessary branches should be chopped off to avoid the loss of moisture. These branches, after being severed from the parent plant, should be stuck into the ground, as it is still possible

for them to develop roots and continue to grow.

It takes some time before a plant collected from a mountain area can resume normal growth. Therefore, such plants should be handled with the utmost care. Plants collected from highly humid areas should be kept humidified, and those collected from arid areas must not be watered too frequently.

Plants newly transplanted from the wilderness should not be overly exposed to sunlight. Exposure to sunlight and the application of fertilizer should be delayed until the emergence of new leaves and the resumption of normal growth. A grower must not be too anxious to view the complicated twists and turns of roots of plants newly collected from mountain areas. These roots need to be protected with soil until much later.

Shaping

Affected by various external factors, plants grown in nature have interesting, sometimes grotesque, features. Conversely, the appearance of potted plants is basically doctored or arranged. Yet, potted plants left on their own can easily develop disorderly branches and must be properly pruned and trimmed. So, shaping is an indispensable part of the cultivation of bonsai plants.

Pruning

The purpose of pruning is to eliminate branches that detract from the beauty and health of a bonsai plant and to stimulate the growth of new leaves and branches. Pruning also helps a plant grow according to the cultivator's wishes. Pruning can be either "heavy" pruning or "light" pruning.

"Heavy" Pruning

In most cases, first-time pruning is heavy pruning. Branches and leaves are extensively pruned away. Heavy pruning is also employed when a cultivator wishes to drastically change the shape of a bonsai. Heavy pruning is practiced only in the spring. During other seasons, plant growth is sluggish and a plant's capacity for healing decreases. Therefore, heavy pruning during any season other than the spring may cause permanent damage to a bonsai.

To carry out heavy pruning, cut off the tip of each branch of a bonsai at a point marking 70 percent of the eventual height of the bonsai when it is fully grown. Make sure the cut is smooth, and cover it with sealant to prevent dehydration and bacterial contamination. Sprouts, and eventually branches, will emerge. When the branches harden somewhat, carefully cut off the old wound, leaving the branches intact. If the bonsai is a plant which produces alternate leaves, slice off the old wound at an angle such that the cut and the new branch line up in a completely straight line. If the bonsai produces opposite leaves, cut out the old wound in a "V" shaped wedge. If one neglects cutting off the old wound, rot might set in.

"Light" Pruning

The purpose of light pruning is to stimulate the growth of new branches. The removal of a branch almost invariably leads to the emergence of new ones. Therefore, if carried out in the correct manner, light pruning is an effective means of getting rid of unhealthy or unwanted branches and encouraging the growth of new and more attractive ones.

One should not go overboard where pruning is concerned, however. Each time a bonsai is pruned, it is wounded and must be given time to recover. Extensive pruning is best limited to once a year, in the spring.

Spring is the season when plants enjoy their greatest period of growth. Pruning is less likely to cause a plant harm if carried out in the spring. Really unattractive or diseased branches can be removed in the fall or winter, however.

A banyan tree stripped of leaves.

The same banyan tree after producing new leaves.

Vigorous growth of bonsai plants after extensive pruning and trimming.

Bud Pinching

An effective way of controlling the growth of branches is bud pinching. This entails the use of the hands or tweezers to pick off unwanted buds from a plant. If a bonsai is allowed to develop freely, branches will emerge from buds all over the plant, making it unruly and messy in appearance. Furthermore, unwanted buds use up nutrients necessary for the growth of desirable branches.

To increase the number of small branches on a bonsai, simply pinch off the buds at the tips of its old branches. New buds and branches will emerge from the sides.

The buds of pine and cypress trees should be pinched off by hand. If one uses a metal utensil, a plant disease, "red-wilt," might develop. One should remove the buds of a pine tree before they have a chance to develop into pine needles. In the case of other species of trees, buds must be pinched off with tweezers before they become mature leaves. As a preventative measure, a bonsai artist can massage the branches of a bonsai from time to time to slow bud production.

Two plants of the same species, one of which has never before been trimmed. The other, potted for seven years, has been subjected to repeated trimming.

New leaves burst out from a newly trimmed branch.

Leaf Trimming

The purpose of leaf trimming is to stimulate the growth of new leaves and to remove unhealthy ones.

The branches and leaves of a bonsai plant must complement one another. This is what gives a bonsai plant its beauty.

The best months for leaf trimming are June and July. Since leaves play an instrumental role in photosynthesis, a plant denuded of all leaves will starve. Therefore, a small amount of fertilizer should be applied to plants selected for leaf trimming about 10 days before removal of the leaves.

It normally takes a plant about 15 days to produce new leaves after trimming. During these 15 days, one can carry out pruning and wiring.

Petioled leaves should be removed by severing the petioles using a pair of scissors. Hand picking could cause damage to the branches. Leaves without petioles should be removed by lifting off leaves by their bases. Before the emergence of new leaves, evaporation takes place at a reduced rate.

Therefore, watering should be correspondingly reduced.

Leaves should be trimmed no more than twice each year. Too much trimming can affect the growth of plants or even kill them.

A Chinese elm in a round shallow pot.

Scars covered by leaves are exposed after a bonsai tree is bared of leaves by pinching.

Wiring

Wiring refers to the use of metal wire to modify the shape of bonsai plants.

Metal wire used in wiring includes copper wire, aluminum wire, and iron wire, as well as others. Strong and non-elastic copper wire is best for the wiring of bonsai plants. It is relatively more expensive, however. Light, inexpensive and moderately strong aluminum wire is widely used. Iron wire is difficult to bend and is rust-prone. Therefore, its use is not recommended. The best months to wire a bonsai plant are February and March. Metal wire can easily eat into the bark in early spring. New branches are very soft and vulnerable. Therefore, a grower must skillfully manipulate the metal wire to prevent the new branches from being damaged. Beginners are advised to carry out wiring in June or July, when new branches have hardened somewhat.

Japanese serissa / exposed-root style / height:13cm(5 inches)/ shallow rectangular vessel

① ②

③

④ ⑤

⑥

58

Wiring procedures.

Scars left by metal wire.

Wiring can produce upright trunks.

The type of wire used varies according to the properties of different plants. Coniferous trees, such as pine and cypress, normally have hardened, non-docile branches and grow at a slow pace. Therefore, modification of their appearance by wiring is difficult and time consuming. When wiring them, copper wire should be used. Before a piece of copper wire can be used, it must be softened by heating. After the appearance of a bonsai plant becomes relatively fixed, the grower should dismantle the copper wiring and remove the verdigris left on the plant using a soft brush. Other trees are relatively more amenable to modification by wiring. One should choose the type of wire used according to the size and properties of each plant. Copper wire is heavier than aluminum wire. Therefore, it should not be used on slanting or precipitously mounted bonsai plants.

The ideal length of a piece of metal wire should be around 1.5 times the length of the branch it is intended to shape.

A bonsai artist should start wiring his bonsai plants as soon as the wire is ready for use. Stick the wire into the soil near the roots of a plant at a 45 degree angle. Hold the plant firm with one hand and use the other hand to wind the wire tightly around the plant in an upward spiral. Pass branches and buds by running the wire above them, not beneath. Tie up the wire by bending its end. Branches are wired in basically the same way. When wiring a bonsai plant, care must be taken to avoid overlapping, lest scars be left on its bark.

If bends are desired, a bonsai artist can gingerly bend the trunks or branches of his bonsai plants. But be careful, as attempts to achieve excessive curvature by force can break them. When modifying the shape of a bonsai plant, do it bit by bit, one step at a time. After making the first attempt, if it does not turn out as planned, wait a little while before giving it another try.

Two or three days before training, gradually reduce watering in order to soften the trugid, hardened branches. This step will help make the work easier. Normal watering should be resumed immediately after training. Because of its hardness, metal wire can easily cause damage to plant tissues if it is not handled with care. Make sure to wrap a soft sheet of paper around a piece of wire before using it in order to reduce friction.

Wiring can give plants with disorderly branches and leaves a brand new appearance. To prevent a piece of metal wire from eating into plant tissues and leaving scars on a plant, a bonsai enthusiast should pay close attention to the growth of the wired plant. After the desired shape is obtained (it takes pine and cypress trees six months to a year to become frozen into a fixed shape, and other trees, one or two months), the wiring should be immediately dismantled. Otherwise, the growth of the plant will be restricted, and death or scarring may result.

Pots

Pot Making

Unglazed pots are usually used as "culture" pots to house newly cultivated plants. Such pots are not intended to have an aesthetic value. Therefore, the clay used in the production of unglazed pots is not refined or finely sifted. Normally, such pots are fired at relatively low temperatures ranging from 800 to 900 degrees centigrade. In most cases, they are mass produced by slurry molding. These pots are usually coarse in texture, inexpensive, permeable, and round in shape.

"Finished product" pots are for housing full-grown bonsai plants. Their production involves more elaborate processes. Such pots can be made either by molding or by hand.

Molding: This means the main production process is slurry molding, which is less costly. The pots are usually crudely glazed. Unnecessary impressions from the molds are often visible on the surface of such pots.

Hand-made pots: Hand-made pots usually have a refined quality and a uniqueness not found in pots made by molding. Production methods vary with shape, be it round or square. Round pots are normally created by the clay biscuit throwing method. After drying, each round-shaped dough form is subjected to polishing. Then, a hole is bored at the bottom of each pre-fired pot, and "foot rims" are carved out and attached to them. After relief carving, the biscuits are fired. The production of square pots involves a far more complicated process. First, five clay sheets are cemented together before a "foot rim" is attached. After polishing and glazing, the biscuits may become deformed because of expansion and contraction. The number of ruined and rejected pots is often very high. Therefore, potters usually turn out roughly prepared biscuits with the help of molds. Following this, they hand-polish the biscuits.

1. Clay biscuit on a potter's wheel.
2. A "finished" biscuit.
3. Pre-glazed biscuits.

Traditional pot making.

1.

2.

3.

1. A terracotta pot.
2. Shallow "cultivation" pots.
3. Standard pots.

Choosing the Right Pot

Potted plants, like caged birds, are confined within a small space. The root system of a potted plant absorbs nutrients from the small amount of soil in which it is anchored. The pot is its home. For this reason, a grower must carefully choose pots that suit the growth patterns of his bonsai plants.

Many kinds of vessels are used to house bonsai plants today. These vessels include earthen pots, clay pots, porcelain pots, plastic pots, and others.

Earthen pots are commonly referred to as unglazed pots. Reddish-brown in color, unglazed pots are plain-looking, highly permeable, easily broken, and inexpensive. They are mainly used for housing "unfinished" bonsai plants.

If the height of a pot is equal to its diameter, such a pot is called a "standard" pot. If the height of a pot is about half of its diameter, it is called a "shallow" pot. Standard pots are normally reserved for seedlings in the initial stage of the cultivation process. Otherwise, shallow pots are preferred by bonsai growers. It must be pointed out that moss easily develops on the surface of earthen pots, thus impeding drainage. Therefore, such pots must be frequently washed.

Glazed pots do not facilitate ventilation, but are attractive. They are easier to clean, but relatively more expensive.

The so-called "iron ore" pots are made from biscuits containing ferrous oxide which are fired at high temperatures. Both their production costs and prices are high. Reddish-brown in color, they look dignified and are highly porous. Beware of bogus goods when purchasing such pots.

Like earthen pots, plastic pots are mainly used to house plants in the process of cultivation. Plastic pots are cheap, light, easy to clean, and are not easily broken. However, they are not porous.

Stone slabs also can be used to house bonsai plants, thus creating special visual effects.

The growth and character of a bonsai is closely related to the pot in which it is housed. Before it is fully grown, a bonsai plant should be housed in a large pot because this facilitates growth. After it matures, it can be transplanted into a "presentation" pot. By this time, rapid growth is unlikely. Therefore, the pot should be just large enough for proper development of the plant's root system. If a small plant is transplanted into a large pot, its branches and leaves will grow profusely and its appearance will be affected.

Exquisitely made pots are themselves objects of art. A beautiful bonsai plant not complemented by a fine pot is like a precious cutlass not cased in an equally precious sheath.

A lot of things are involved in the selection of pots. From a practical point of view, it is first necessary to determine the intended use for a pot. For the cultivation of scions, it is necessary to use large and porous pots. As the shape of a plant approaches the desired form, a scion may be transplanted to a large, unglazed pot. By the time a plant becomes full-grown, one can switch to a pot just big enough for a root system to develop.

Without a drainage hole, a vessel cannot be called a top-grade pot no matter how exquisite its design and quality. Drainage holes are an important part of glazed earthen or porcelain pots. These pots are not porous and the drainage holes at their bottoms are the only conduit to drain away excess water. Drainage holes are usually found at the bottom or lowest point of a pot. Pots with depressions retain water and may cause roots to rot. One should not choose pots with drainage holes which are

Boccaro pot.

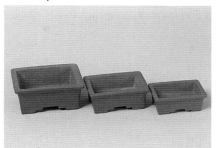

A Kiyomizu-yaki pot (L) and a celadon pot.

Clay pots.

too close to the ground.

Shallow pots usually have more drainage holes—at least 10—at the bottom.

A pot should have foot rims. Pots without foot rims must have at least two drainage openings. Otherwise, not only is water unable to come out because of atmospheric pressure, but also dust and filth can easily accumulate. The inner surface of a pot should be unglazed. Otherwise, roots cannot develop properly and cannot be properly anchored.

A hand-made pot.

1. Chien-lung period (1736-1795) glazed pots.
2. A set of red clay pots.
3. Drum-like red clay pots.
4. Ming Dynasty vessels.
5. Red clay pot (L) and dark clay pot.
6. Wenshan ware, coated with iron oxide before firing.

1.

2.

3.

4.

5.

6.

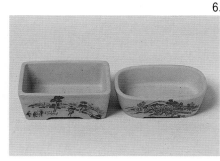

63

A trident maple in a hand-made gourd-shaped vessel.

A bonsai plant housed in a stub-shaped vessel.

Specially designed bonsai plant housed in a specially designed pot.

Potting

Pots are to bonsai plants what clothes are to people. Whether a bonsai plant is beautiful or not depends to a large extent on the pot in which it is housed.

Bonsai trees with straight, upright trunks should be housed in shallow pots that are either oval or rectangular in shape. Thus potted, the bonsai give one the impression that they are columns supporting the sky. Bonsai plants with slanting trunks should be housed in deep pots to convey the idea of unyielding steadfastness. Saplings planted in small pots look slender and graceful. Branched plants grown in clusters should be housed in large and shallow vessels to create a quasi-natural atmosphere. They also can be potted in tall, slender vessels to make up for the absence of a main trunk. Cascade style bonsai plants can be potted in two different ways. They can be housed in heavy-set containers, so that the pots will look like cliffs with leaves and branches draping over them. Or they can be housed in small, shallow pots, so that the branches of the

bonsai plants will form drooping canopies larger than the pots. "Rock planting" bonsai plants should be housed in pots made of materials similar to the rock to create a holistic impression. Bonsai plants with exposed roots should be housed in flat, shallow vessels to highlight the beauty of their roots. Traces of battles against the elements may be found on bonsai trees deliberately left withered. Such bonsai should be housed in plain, ancient-looking pots in dull colors. "Forest-style" bonsai are preferably housed in large, shallow vessels or on smooth flat stone slabs. In this way, their appearance is "softened" and they look more natural. Pines and cypresses are evergreen trees and should be housed in "iron ore pots" made of heavy-set clay. Deciduous trees change appearance during the four seasons. In spring and summer, they are luxuriantly green. In autumn, they display a variety of colors. And in winter, all the leaves are gone and only their branches remain. When choosing pots for them, it is

Household utensils also can be used as bonsai pots.

A vessel made from a pot shard.

dwarf mulberry tree / raft style / height :8cm(3 inches)

necessary to avoid colors closely resembling the leaves of the bonsai plants they are intended to house. Like deciduous trees, trees which produce flowers and fruit should not be contained in vessels of colors similar to those of their flowers and fruit. Herbs are preferably housed in vivid and elegantly designed pots, in order to accentuate their vitality. Small bonsai plants should be kept in brightly colored porcelain China pots to stress their delicate beauty. Normally, bonsai plants are placed at the center of circular or rectangular vessels. Plants may be placed to the left or right of the center in rectangular or elliptical vessels. In such vessels, more space should be left in front of the plants than behind them in order to enhance their overall appearance.

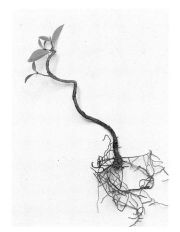

The same plant housed in different pots.

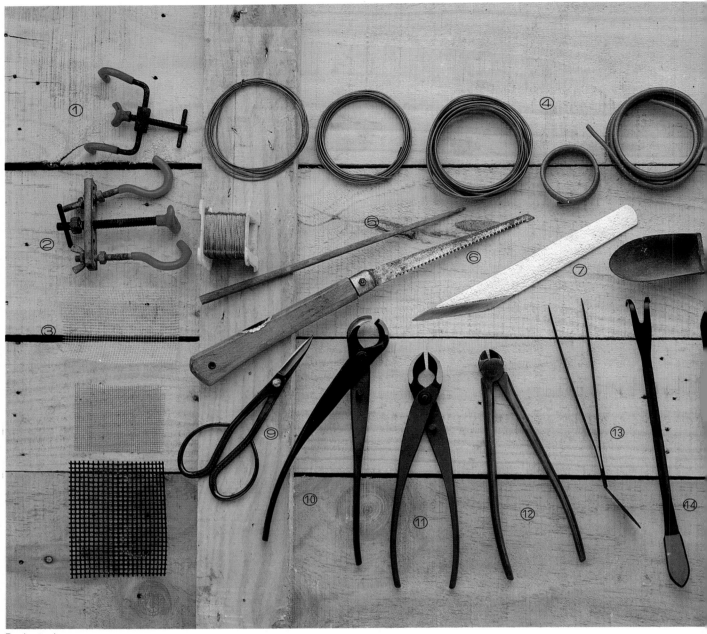

Basic tools.

Watering jugs.

Tools

As with any other hobby, possessing just the right tools is the secret to success in bonsai cultivation. Each tool should be a pleasure to work with.

The following tools are the bare essentials necessary for shaping and training bonsai.

Tweezers with pointed tips: Used to pluck weeds, pick off insects, remove withered leaves, and unravel tangled wire. Most tweezers have a flattened head which comes in handy for leveling soil or laying moss.

Wire cutters: After a bonsai becomes fixed in shape with the help of wire, the

1. Device for bending branches.
2. Device for bending large branches.
3. Wire screens.
4. Wire.
5. Stick.
6. Miniature saw.
7. Grafting knife.
8. Miniature shovel.
9. Short-handled branch cutter.
10. Round-bladed branch cutter.
11. Oval-bladed cutter.
12. Wire cutter.
13. Tweezers.
14. Miniature rake.
15. Pinchers with pointed tips (for stripping bark).
16. Long-handled branch cutter.
17. Wire cutter (for removing wire from small branches).

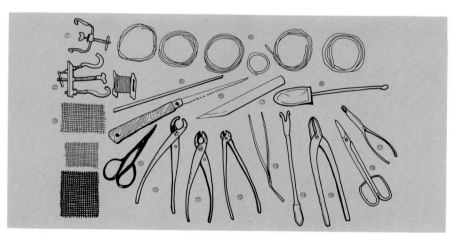

wire holding the branches in place must be removed. Sometimes it can be unraveled by hand, but usually it is easier to cut it with a wire cutter. When using a wire cutter, beware of accidentally nicking the bark of the bonsai.

Forked branch cutter: Forked branch cutters have two curved blades which make cutting easy and leave smoothly cut surfaces.

Small branch cutter: This is the most frequently used tool in the cultivation of bonsai. It is absolutely essential for cutting small branches, trimming leaves, and removing buds.

Some bonsai artists prefer to have two small branch cutters, one with a long handle and one with a short handle. The long-handled tool is used to probe among dense growths of branches. Never use small branch cutters to cut large branches or roots, lest you damage the tool and leave an uneven cut surface.

Grafting knife: In addition to grafting, this type of knife comes in handy for smoothing cut surfaces, layering, and creating shari style bonsai (bonsai with a section of bark removed). Layering is a very difficult process, and using an ordinary knife, which may leave an uneven cut surface, will prevent a cutting from fitting tightly to a stock, thus slowing down the healing process. A grafting knife, however, has a very firm and sharp blade, and makes smooth cuts that allow a cutting and stock to be bound tightly together.

Apart from these basic tools, some bonsai artists employ tiny rakes to disentangle roots, sticks for shoving soil in the spaces between roots, a miniature saw for cutting hard wood, and a pair of pinchers with a pointed tip for stripping bark and wiring trees. If one wants to be really extravagant, one can also purchase a soil thermometer, a hydrogrometer, an acidity-akalinity gauge, and so forth.

Re-Potting

Re-potting is an important step in the process of bonsai cultivation. One reason why re-potting is necessary is that with the passage of time, the roots of a bonsai absorb all the nutrients from the soil in which they are planted. As a result, the soil becomes acidic or alkaline, thus affecting the growth of the bonsai. Another reason is that if roots are constricted in a small container with no room to expand, they may wither and die. Or, as sometimes happens, in their desperate search for a new source of nutrients, they will burst through the side of a pot.

A small bonsai plant should be repotted at least every two years. Some species, such as fast-growing shrubs, need to be relocated to new, larger pots once a year. Slow-growing coniferous trees, on the other hand, can last three to four years between re-pottings.

Besides the actual relocation of a plant to a new pot, re-potting also refers to such work as trimming and pruning branches, sorting out roots, replacing soil, and making placement adjustments.

To determine whether or not the time is right for re-potting, one should examine the drainage holes at the pot's bottom to check if roots are peeking through. If so, relocation to a larger pot is necessary. Another indicator that re-potting is in order is the emergence of root hairs from topsoil. If a bonsai suddenly exhibits a marked decrease in the rate of growth, this is also a sign.

A Japanese mahonia with exposed roots.

Healthy roots should have a great deal of root hair.

Re-potting procedures.

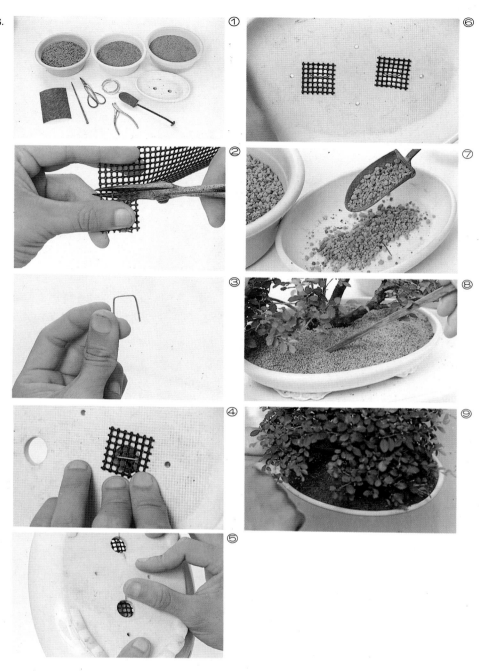

The following are the procedures for re-potting:

1. If a bonsai is being trained with metal wire, first remove the wire.
2. Lift the pot and gently tap along its rim to loosen the soil.
3. Remove the plant from the pot. Sort out the root system, remove soil stuck to the roots, cut off rotten roots and redundant branches, and clip off one third of the length of the longer branches and roots.
4. Select a suitable pot and arrange a piece of wire mesh across its drainage hole.
5. Place a layer of coarse-grained soil on top of the mesh.
6. Fill up one third of the pot with medium-grained soil.
7. Put the bonsai in the pot with its roots evenly spread out. Make sure that the roots are not touching the inner surface of the pot.
8. Sprinkle fine-grained soil over the roots.
9. Using a stick, fill the spaces between the roots with soil in order to firmly anchor the roots and facilitate drainage. This will also prevent harmful insects from penetrating into the soil.
10. Put the pot into a basin of water so that water can seep up into the soil through the drainage hole at its bottom. Remove any impurities that are discernable on the moistened soil.

If the bonsai to be re-potted is of the cascade style, use a tall vessel and allow the roots of the bonsai to droop naturally before adding fine-grained soil. If planting a bonsai in a shallow basin, rather than packing soil tightly around the roots to keep the plant from falling over, employ metal wire or a prop to keep it firmly in place.

After re-potting, the plant should be protected from strong sunlight or strong wind for two weeks. When new buds appear, the plant has begun a new life cycle.

69

Bonsai plants on display.

Buying Bonsai

Most bonsai enthusiasts are captivated by the thought of creating their own living work of art from scratch. Unfortunately, because time is in such limited supply these days, few can actually realize this desire. Most bonsai artists content themselves with buying finished or semi-finished bonsai.

When buying bonsai, carefully consider each potential purchase. Bonsai are not cheap, and a bad buy will only waste time and money but also cause great disappointment.

Before purchasing any finished bonsai, check for scars on the trunk or branches that may be hidden beneath leaves. Check also for signs of the presence of insects or scars caused by improper wiring. In addition, take a look at the bottom of the bonsai pot to see if the soil is muddy, which is an indication that the bonsai was watered improperly and might have rotten roots as a result. In the case of pine and cypress trees,

A Ming Dynasty picture showing a bonsai stall.

Bonsai on display in Taipei's Flower Market.

Buyers examine target purchases carefully.

A happy bonsai enthusiast returns home with purchases.

the mildew-like growths surrounding the drainage holes of the pots housing them are not a sign of disease, but instead are a distinctive form of fungi normally present in these species.

After all these procedures, one can begin haggling. Bonsai plants are most often priced according to their size. However, there are big but plain-looking and small yet beautiful bonsai.

If one wishes to buy semi-finished bonsai, a wide range of choices is available. One advantage to buying semi-finished bonsai is that they are usually reasonably priced.

When choosing bonsai, one must take care to avoid plants with scarred or wounded branches, roots, and leaves. Yet, one should not readily reject plants with "healable"

wounds. Plants with indelible scars (such as those caused by wiring), swellings caused by improper layering, and wounds on their trunks are best discarded.

According to dealers, during "hibernation," deciduous trees are not marketable. Beginners usually will look askance at their naked and forlorn branches. In reality, trees bared of leaves reveal their strong points and shortcomings. Therefore, inexperienced bonsai enthusiasts should seize this golden opportunity to make purchases. If this is not possible, one can ask reliable dealers and sellers for recommendations.

An advantage to purchasing semi-finished bonsai is that one can supplement one's collection with special or locally unavailable species. Therefore, it is

bird-lime holly / shari style / height:48cm(19 inches) / oval vessel

Bonsai plants with wiring scars on their bark are a bad purchase.

necessary to pay attention to post-purchase care, so that the newly purchased plant will not lose its distinctive qualities as a result of acclimatization.

In addition to buying semi-finished bonsai, one can also buy a bonsai stub and wait for it to produce buds. For people denied the pleasure of growing their plants in countryside nurseries or seedbeds, stubs are a good purchase.

Buyers should avoid bonsai plants with open wounds, such as this banyan tree.

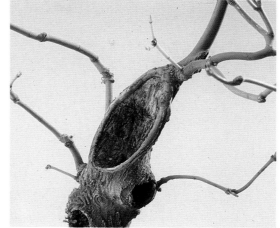

Here is a badly scarred plant. Although careful cultivation has made it possible for the plant to produce new branches around the scarred area , chances are slim that the scar can ever be completely healed.

A well-chosen pot greatly enhances the beauty of a bonsai. As a result, the price of a bonsai has a lot to do with the pot it is contained in. These days, one can purchase pots with prices ranging from a few dollars to several hundred dollars. Many bonsai enthusiasts wrongly assume that pots are nothing more than a temporary habitat for their plant. They refuse to "waste" time and money on selecting and purchasing a proper vessel. But in fact, a bonsai is a living work of art. Bonsai enthusiasts should take advantage of the entire bonsai "work," including the pot, to create a thing of beauty.

Before purchasing a bonsai with a profusion of branches and leaves, first peer through the leaves to inspect the trunk. Sometimes such bonsai have scarred trunks which are hidden by branches and leaves, A bonsai of this type may still be worth purchasing, but you should pay a relatively lower price for it.

This plant has obviously gone through a process of careful cultivation to allow it to produce an attractive network of branches. Upon close inspection, however, one can see that the two forks of the trunk have been chopped off at a flat angle and are not very attractive.

Creation
Trees and plants

Pine

Many bonsai artists choose pine as the basic material for their artistic expression. Among the several types of pine used in bonsai cultivation are black pine, five needle pine and corticata pine. Each of these has its own advantages and disadvantages from the standpoint of bonsai cultivation. Black pine is easy to work with because it can endure cold and dry weather conditions. Five needle pine thrives at high elevations, and corticata pine is suitable for an arid habitat.

If cultivating a pine bonsai starting from a seed, plant the seed during the first two weeks of March. If the weather is warm, the seed should sprout in 10 days. After cotyledons (seed leaves) begin to appear, trim the seed's tap roots and transplant it into a pot. From this point on, cultivate the seedling as you would any other bonsai.

Raising a pine bonsai from a seed is not difficult, but it is time consuming. Sometimes it is to one's advantage to buy pine nursery stock that is about three years old. One should choose nursery stock that is short and thick, with fully developed lateral roots and thick growths of small leaves. After two or three more years of cultivation, a mature bonsai will emerge.

In order to shape the bonsai, one should pinch off undesirable buds each spring, just after they begin to emerge. Pinch off small and weak buds as well, so that normal buds will have a better chance to develop. In order to encourage branch growth in a certain direction, leave buds which are growing in the desired direction intact and pinch off those growing in other directions.

red pine / literati, slanting / height:12cm(5 inches) / drum-like vessel

Prune pine trees with caution. Wounds created by pruning ooze sticky sap, causing a loss of the tree's nutrients, thus slowing down the healing process. When pruning, avoid making large cuts. Do not prune branches all the way down to the trunk. Instead make a cut about halfway and wait for the branch to wither somewhat before cutting off the rest. Do not prune off all superfluous wood. If some is left on the bonsai, it will become more hardy.

A pine tree grows very slowly, so it is best to wait until it is about three years old before beginning to transform it into a

bonsai. When transplanting a pine, lay down a layer of pebbles in the bottom of the new pot to prevent the accumulation of stagnant water. Do not shake off all the old soil surrounding the roots, and be sure to leave the grayish fungus attached to them intact. The presence of this fungus is essential if the pine is to survive.

For a vessel, choose an unglazed or earthenware pot of a dull color. It will suit the steadfast and simple appearance of the pine bonsai. A pot with a thick and heavy bottom is especially suitable for pine presentation.

This grotesquely shaped clump of juniper trees has been bent and twisted by natural elements.

Juniper

Juniper is another popular material for use in bonsai cultivation. Oriental arborvita and sargent juniper are often used to create small bonsai. Sargent juniper exhibits great vitality and has a pleasant shape. It grows so slowly that after hundreds of years, exposed to the cold, and battered by rain, wind and snow, some trees barely reach a height of four feet.

The roots of a juniper are thin and tender. When pruning them, cut as few as possible. Although juniper grown in the wild can endure the bright sun and arid conditions, those cultivated in pots should be treated with the same consideration as other bonsai. Do not expose them to direct sunlight, and make sure they are adequately watered. Do not water a juniper too much, however, as this will cause its leaves to become distorted during growth, thus reducing the bonsai's value as a viewing object.

Sargent juniper react well to propagation by cutting. In order to reshape, bend the branches of a juniper with the help of metal wire. One should use one's imagination to create unusual shapes and designs for both the branches and the trunk of a juniper bonsai.

If one wishes to cultivate a shari style bonsai, one should wait until spring to begin stripping bark. Avoid pruning during the winter, as cuts will heal very slowly. In the summer, juniper bonsai have a tendency to dry up, so make sure that each tree is watered regularly.

Like pine, juniper bonsai ooze thick sap when cut. Avoid using pruning shears or knives on a juniper except for first time pruning. It is better to pinch off unwanted buds by hand. To encourage lateral growth, pinch off buds that emerge at the tips of branches.

fragrant maple / upright / height: 14cm(5.5 inches) / shallow rectangular vessel

Chinese sweet gum

Chinese sweet gum bonsai are easy to cultivate and shape, and thus are an excellent material for beginners. This type of tree is thick and strong, with sweet-smelling leaves. After reaching maturity, cracks appear along the trunk and branches of Chinese sweet gum, creating a grizzled and weathered look that is quite pleasing.

There are a number of advantages to working with Chinese sweet gum. It is strong and hardy, and can stand a great deal of pruning without being adversely affected. Its branches are pliable and easily shaped with wire. In addition, it buds easily and new branches grow quickly even after heavy pruning. Most importantly, Chinese sweet gum is a fast growing species.

The best method of propagation for Chinese sweet gum is air layering, as the survival rate of cuttings is not high. If cultivating this species from a seed, plant the seed in February or March.

Like the maple, the leaves of a Chinese sweet gum change color in the fall.

77

Maple

As far as deciduous trees go, there is no better material for bonsai cultivation than maple. The shape of a maple's branches, the color of its leaves, and the arrangement of its root base are all quite extraordinary. As such, its value in bonsai cultivation is unequaled.

Finished maple bonsai exhibit a number of interesting variations. Maple leaves may have three, five, seven or nine points. They are green, red or multi-colored, according to the season. Branches grow vertically, horizontally, or droop down.

Most artificially created hybrid maples are incapable of self-propagation and must be reproduced through grafting. Grafting is carried out from February to late March. Mountain maple is the most commonly used stock material.

Maple leaves and branches are more difficult to cultivate than those of the Chinese sweet gum. Yet, a maple's potential for root development is astonishing. Consequently, maple is an excellent choice for the cultivation of exposed-root, root-over-rock and twisted-root style bonsai.

Maple bark is tender, so when employing metal wire to shape branches, make sure to first wrap the wire in cotton paper so that scars and marks are not left on the maple's surface.

Cultivate maple in a spotlessly clean environment. Water a maple bonsai regularly and protect it from direct sunlight. If one provides a little extra fertilizer to a maple during early fall, its leaves will turn a more brilliant red later on. About the time that a maple is ready to shed its leaves, one should provide it with a little extra water to keep the leaves from turning brown, withering, or falling off before becoming completely red. Just after the bonsai sheds its leaves, spray it with a mixture of lime and sulfur in a one-time application to prevent the onset of powdery mildew disease come spring.

trident maple / exposed-root style/ height:18cm(7 inches) / shallow rectangular earthenware pot
(right) Japanese mountain maple/ coiled-trunk / height:8cm(3 inches)/ round earthenware pot

Japanese red maple / twin-trunk
height:17cm(7 inches) / hand-made vessel

Chinese elm

Beginning bonsai enthusiasts often are unable to distinguish between a Chinese elm and a Japanese elm. In fact, although they may look similar at first glance, they are not alike at all. Chinese elm trees have small oval-shaped leaves with thick sinuses, and their branches naturally grow in a straight line. Japanese elm, on the other hand, have larger leaves with thinner sinuses, and branches that grow in a zig-zag pattern.

Chinese elm branches are inclined to grow horizontally, making them an ideal material for the cultivation of layered bonsai. Regular pruning is a necessity with Chinese elm because its small and thickly growing leaves prevent fresh air from penetrating to the inner branches and trunk of the tree, thus causing them to slowly wither. When the leaves begin to shed during winter, be sure to clean off any that fall upon the branches, otherwise they will decay and cause the death of the bonsai.

Chinese elm is easily cultivated from a cutting. All one has to do is take a healthy part of a root from an elm tree sometime around March, and bury it under loose-grained soil with its top slightly exposed. After about one month, it should sprout. Chinese elm grows quickly, and within a year of planting, the roots of the cutting will have spread all throughout its container. With young Chinese elm, it is necessary to re-pot frequently. As older Chinese elm grow more slowly, they need to be re-potted only every two or three years.

Chinese elm / root- over-rock / height of rock:12cm(5 inches) / yellow hexagonal container

Chinese elm / coiled-trunk / height:11cm (4.5 inches) / hand-made earthenware vessel

79

Japanese gray-bark elm/ upright / height:23cm(9 inches) / shallow elliptical pot

Japanese gray-bark elm

Japanese gray-bark elm is an excellent material for the creation of upright style bonsai. Of all the broad-leaved trees, elm lives the longest. As a result, venerable old elm trees, preserved in the form of bonsai, are found everywhere.

Japanese gray-bark elm roots are naturally inclined to grow horizontally, forming a strong and steady base for the upward growth of the tree. Branches grow straight up towards the heavens. A perfectly cultivated Japanese gray-bark elm will look just like an upside-down broom.

Japanese gray-bark elm branches grow rapidly and profusely, especially from spring until the end of summer. They produce giant leaves, as well as unnecessary buds which must be pinched off regularly to prevent the bonsai from ending up thick at the top and thin at the bottom.

In order to cultivate a Japanese gray-bark elm bonsai, purchase an upright nursery stock and cut off its lower branches. Then trim off the tap roots because an upright style bonsai like elm should be planted in a shallow basin to accentuate its unique character. As it is often difficult to locate a completely straight nursery stock, it will probably be necessary to use metal wire to shape the tree while it is young. In the early period of cultivation, apply extra fertilizer to speed up the finalization of the trunk shape. When the bark begins to bulge around the metal wire, it is time to remove the wire from the bonsai. The marks left by the wire will gradually disappear as the bonsai continues to grow.

After the shape of the trunk is fixed, trim away any disorderly branches. Whenever undesirable buds appear, pinch them off immediately to allow other branches to grow. After three or four years of cultivation, the bonsai should be relocated to a more permanent decorative pot.

80

banyan / coiled-trunk / height:14cm (5.5 inches) / rectangular celadonware

Banyan trees are found everywhere in dry and hot regions. They are beautiful and majestic.

Banyan

Banyan is a sub-tropical broad-leaved evergreen tree that thrives in dry and hot conditions. It is so sensitive to cold that its leaves fall off in chilly weather, and it dies if placed in a low-temperature environment for any period of time. Yet, banyan is tenacious and can grow even in the cracks of a wall. Nursery stock will blossom into a graceful bonsai. Except during chilly weather, any time is suitable for taking a cutting. Banyan also can be cultivated from a seed. But this method tends to make banyan roots swell like a potato, and is therefore not suitable for small bonsai.

Banyan bonsai are easy to care for and can be kept indoors for viewing. It is not necessary to regularly change banyan pots.

A natural root-over-rock style banyan.

Azalea

There exist both evergreen and deciduous azalea bushes. An azalea's flowering period varies according to species, climate and cultivation method. Among hybrid species, the oldham azalea is commonly used as stock material for grafting. Among wild azalea species, reptile azalea is the most popular. The branches of a reptile azalea bend and twist in amazing directions.

Azalea roots are thin, well-developed and capable of absorbing huge amounts of fertilizer. When planted in a shallow pot filled with slightly acidic soil, azaleas form an excellent root base. Each year, after the plant flowers, prune and fertilize it. Get rid of dying flowers to keep them from consuming plant nutrients needed by healthier buds.

Six months before the flowering season, prune off undesirable branches. Soon after pruning, new leaf buds will sprout from pruned branches and they must be pinched off lest they harm future blossoming. Do not add too much fertilizer during this period or flower buds will change into leaf buds.

Azaleas like moisture. After flower buds appear, increase the amount of water you are supplying, and make sure that the plant receives ample sunlight, as this will enable it to produce fuller blossoms. During the flowering season, one may move the plant indoors for viewing, but only to a spot with plenty of ventilation and sunlight. If the flowers begin to wither, move the plant outside again.

azalea / coiled-trunk / height 8cm(3 inches) / dark red square vessel

Rhododendron have been cultivated in China for over a thousand years. They are valued for their gorgeous flowers.

azalea / twin-trunk / height:8cm(3 inches) / fringed square container
azalea / slanting / height:11cm(4.5 inches) / round earthenware pot

An azalea in full bloom.

Japanese serissa / exposed-root style / height:18cm(7 inches) / round clay pot

Japanese serissa / coiled-trunk / height:20cm(8 inches) / shallow vessel

Japanese serissa / coiled-trunk / height:18cm(7 inches)/ shallow vessel

Japanese Serissa

Japanese serissa is a popular material for bonsai cultivation. It has either completely green leaves, green leaves with white edges, or white leaves with small green patches. The kind with completely green leaves is the easiest to take care of. Japanese serissa flower in early summer. Flower buds are usually found at the base of petioles of leaves that emerge from young branches. Old branches do not produce flower buds.

To propagate a Japanese serissa, take a cutting of any part of the plant, especially its roots. Plant the cutting in soil that is not sticky, and keep it shaded until it matures enough to start producing buds. A few months after buds begin to emerge, the cutting will mature into a young Japanese serissa.

A Japanese serissa grows very quickly, so make sure to add fertilizer to the soil occasionally to ensure that it does not become depleted of nutrients. If any branches or leaves start to wither, remove them immediately and allow the plant to absorb a little more sunlight.

Bamboo

Bamboo is very difficult to dwarf, and so is not commonly used in bonsai cultivation. With advanced gardening techniques, however, it is possible to create beautiful miniature bamboo bonsai.

Plant bamboo bonsai in sandy soil which is rich in organic substances. Keep bamboo in a well-lit location.

To create a dwarfed bamboo, do not simply cut off the upper part of a bamboo plant. This will create an unattractive plant. Instead, remove the newly developed bud stems located beneath the ground. Plant them in a new container. Add organic fertilizer and avoid over-watering.

When trimming, remove only really disorderly branches and leave the rest intact. A bamboo should have a sort of wild beauty about it.

dwarf bamboo / forest style / height of tallest plant:7cm(2 inches)/ rectangular shallow pot

85

(left) mulberry tree / shari style / width:15 cm(6 inches) / glazed hexagonal pot
(right) mulberry tree / raft style / twin-trunk/ height:9cm(3.5 inches) / shallow oval vessel

A mulberry tree found in a natural environment.

Mulberry

Mulberry is a deciduous tree marked by grayish-white spots on its bark and stripes on its roots. When planting a mulberry bonsai, keep part of the roots exposed if possible, as they add color to the overall appearance of the tree.

Mulberry trees have a difficult time producing new branches, but what branches they have are usually sturdy and strong. When pruning, trim all the buds except for two off of each branch so that nutrients won't be wasted on the production of undesirable twigs.

The thick bark of a mulberry is easily damaged. When pruning, use razor-sharp double-blade pruners so that the bark is not accidentally torn off.

Mulberry trees are often victimized by harmful insects and diseases. In spring, mulberry trees are prone to powdery mildew disease. At all times of the year, however, one should watch out for insects and diseases.

Cutting is the easiest method of propagation for mulberry bonsai. One can take a cutting from even a large branch, and prepare it thusly: wait for the cutting's sap to dry, then stand it up in sandy soil and expose it to sunlight for half of each day. After one month, roots should begin to develop.

Mulberry trees are adapted to arid conditions, so avoid over-watering. Too much water will cause the branches of a mulberry to grow crazily. If you wish to deepen the colors of the fruit produced by your mulberry bonsai, add a little phosphoric fertilizer to the soil.

(left) crape myrtle (Lagerstroemia indica) / coiled-trunk / height:9cm(3.5 inches) / hand-made clay bowl

(right) crape myrtle (Lagerstroemia indica) / slanting / height:15cm(6 inches) / square vessel

The Crape Myrtle

The crape myrtle is identifiable by its alternately growing leaves. It flowers in the summer, producing purple, white and red flowers. Wild species of crape myrtle do not equal the beauty of cultivated ones and are used solely for cross-breeding rather than for bonsai cultivation.

As a crape myrtle ages, its bark will gradually fall off until it is totally denuded. The trunk will then become silky smooth.

Plant a crape myrtle in porous soil to prevent its roots from rotting. Expose the plant to plenty of sunlight, otherwise its leaves will turn yellow and fall off and it will produce no flowers. When wiring, cushion the wire with cloth to prevent scarring of the bark.

A crape myrtle continues to produce new buds even in old age. Its leaves will turn orange in the fall season if the plant is provided with enough nutrients.

To propagate a crape myrtle, one can choose between sowing a seed, layering, and cutting. In general, these plants are good for beginning bonsai enthusiasts as they require very little care.

Fukien tea / exposed-root, slanting-trunk / height:17cm(7 inches) / round vessel

A Fukien tea tree laden with fruit.

Fukien Tea

The Fukien tea plant is an evergreen shrub which features small leaves with dentate (saw-toothed) edges. It produces small white flowers in the spring and red fruit after the flowering season. It is indigenous to central and southern Taiwan.

Although this plant can adapt itself to poorly lit habitats, it grows best in areas where it receives plenty of sunshine. Fukien tea grows quite rapidly, and responds well to the application of slow-working organic fertilizer once every two months. The application of concentrated, fast-acting chemical fertilizers is not recommended, as this can cause over-growth and distortion of the plant's branches and leaves.

To train a Fukien tea plant, shape its limbs with the help of metal wire. Wiring is only effective with young, tender branches, however, as older ones become fixed in place and may break if bent too drastically.

The most common method of propagation of these plants is cutting. Put cuttings in sandy soil and cultivate as you would other plants. Be sure to apply disinfectants to the wounds left on the parent plant by cutting.

Fukien tea plants cannot endure cold weather. If left outside during the winter, their leaves will turn black and fall off, and even the tips of their roots will wither.

Fukien tea plants have long, flexible roots, making them the perfect material for the creation of a "cling-to-rock" style bonsai.

Fukien tea / coiled-trunk / height:6cm(2.5 inches) / jar-shaped vessel

Taiwan fire-thorn / exposed-root style / slanting / height:22cm(9 inches) / round clay

Taiwan Fire-thorn

The Taiwan fire-thorn displays dense growths of green leaves and laterally growing branches. Its branches and twigs are thorned. The most beautiful part of the plant is its fruit, which grows in clusters.

The plant has adapted to a dry habitat and does not require much water. One should keep the soil in which a Taiwan fire-thorn is planted moistened only. Excessive watering will lead to the growth of unwanted branches and will cause the fruit to fall off. Trim a Taiwan fire-thorn in March and again in June or July of each year. One need not apply much fertilizer to the plant, but if it runs low on nutrients, the number of leaves and fruit it produces will decrease. From April to October, apply a small amount of fertilizer to the plant every four weeks.

When trimming the plant in June or July, snip off all but one or two of the fruit. Otherwise, the fruit will use up the lion's share of the nutrients absorbed by the plant, causing the plant to grow less vigorously the following year.

The two most common methods of Fukien tea propagation are sowing a seed and layering. If one wishes to create a very small bonsai, cutting is also effective.

89

white dragon grass / height: 14cm
(5.5 inches) / shallow pot

Herbs

Herbs are rarely used as material for the creation of bonsai. This is because they appear less majestic as bonsai than do most other bonsai materials. Yet, herbs have a certain raw vitality and grace that other plants lack.

ivy vines / cascade style / height of vessel:17cm(7 inches)

The Chinese brake thrives in a cool, humid environment.

Chinese brake / clump style / height:10 cm(4 inches) / hand-made clay pot

Chinese Brake

Chinese brake is a colorful evergreen fern. The most common method of propagation of this fern is separation.

One can also collect Chinese brake from the wild. To do so, dig up the plant, keeping its roots intact, and trim off its upper leaves. Then plant it in a suitable container. A Chinese brake should be left in a cool, shaded area and be provided with enough water to keep the soil it is planted in properly moistened. Chinese brake cannot stand being left in direct sunlight.

To preserve the water-absorbing properties of soil, one can mix it with some organic fertilizer and spagnum-moss cut into tiny pieces. Avoid excessive watering of Chinese brake, especially during the winter, as this will lower the temperature of the soil and harm the plant.

dwarf sweet-rush / root-over-rock / height of rock:3.5cm(1.5 inches) / bronze tray

Sweet-rush

This evergreen grass usually plays a supporting role in bonsai cultivation. It is planted alongside other bonsai as an added attraction. Sweet-rush is either completely green in color, or green with white or yellow stripes.

This grass should be planted in moistened soil that is not sticky. One can add a small amount of nitrogenous fertilizer to the soil every so often to make the leaves of the grass shinier. It can be left indoors, provided that it is placed in a well-lit area. Do not overexpose sweet-rush to sunlight, or its leaves will turn yellow and wither away.

The most effective and common method of propagation of this grass is separation. After planting a scion, roots will quickly develop. Trimming is not required for sweet-rush.

This grass may also be cultivated in water. Just be sure to keep its environment

dwarf sweet-rush / root-over-rock / height of rock:2cm
(0.8 inches) / oval vessel

cactus / group planting / height of the tallest plant:12cm(5 inches) / leaf-shaped pot

Cactus plants of different species create a "desert" atmosphere when planted together.

spotlessly clean.

Cactus

A cactus is not cared for in the same way as are other bonsai. Cacti prefer loose, sandy soil, and have weak roots, so as a result they have a penchant for falling over. Bonsai enthusiasts must prop up their cacti with stones placed around the base of each plant. Another method of preventing cacti from tipping over is to plant them in a small pot, and then bury the pot itself in another container of soil.

Cacti must be given space to grow and mature. Once they have matured, they are easy to care for, as they require no training or trimming. They are long-lived and relatively free of pests. As long as they are located in a well-lit area and are rearranged from time to time, there should be no real danger of them dying. Do not over-water a cactus, as this will cause its roots to rot.

A variety of cacti can be planted in a large, flat container, combined with sand, pebbles, and stones, to create a wonderful little desert scene.

93

A single rock, a single tree and dense moss in a wide and large pot create a vision of wilderness.

Creating Your Own Bonsai

Bonsai is a process by which nature is transformed into art. It entails the reshaping of nature's materials to create a living, growing art work, bound only by human imagination and talent.

Virtually any tree or plant found in nature can be used as a basic material for bonsai cultivation. Depending upon the raw material selected, a bonsai enthusiast can choose between many different forms of propagation, including sowing seeds, cutting, layering, grafting, and separation.

The central tenet of bonsai cultivation is that a plant or tree removed from nature, and transformed into an object of art, must be miniaturized without having its wild spirit and vitality affected. Some species are simply too large and coarse to be miniaturized without appearing incongruous or ridiculous.

When planting a seedling or nursery stock, take into account its future shape and special characteristics. For example, a tree with strong roots will probably be suited to the creation of a root-over-rock style bonsai. A trailing or sinuous plant might make a wonderful cascade style bonsai. Trees which have strong roots and branches can be cultivated into multi-trunk bonsai. For a shari style bonsai, use a tree with great flexibility and tenacity. When creating a literati style bonsai, you will have the best results if you start with a tree that naturally grows straight and upright. Research the growth patterns of trees and plants in nature to determine what style of bonsai they are most suited to become.

The slowest method of propagating a bonsai is sowing a seed. Yet, in bonsai jargon, such bonsai are called "proper bonsai" and are greatly prized. Cutting, layering, separating, and grafting might have faster results, but in the end there is no feeling quite like viewing a bonsai one has shaped and trained from a shapeless seed into an elegant and attractive living art work.

A nursery stock that has a natural tendancy to grow upright should be planted in the center of a vessel. Others should be planted so that they are slightly slanted in order to enable their roots to grow more evenly and orderly. Once roots have developed, they can be replanted according to the style of bonsai they are to become.

If a bonsai tree is planted in a deep vessel, its upper branches will develop more rapidly than its lower ones. Eventually the bonsai might become top heavy. If this occurs, use a metal wire to readjust the shape of the lower branches. Then prune the upper branches and leaves. Continue to regularly prune them until the lower branches match the upper branches in thickness and length.

The secret to creating dense growths of small branches is to repeatedly trim them.

Trim upward growing branches to force them to grow horizontally and to produce a greater number of smaller branches.

Trimming methods vary between species. In general, however, try to preserve the topmost bud on a branch so that it can continue to lengthen, while trimming off all the buds along its sides. Eventually, two new branches will emerge from the single remaining bud. When these two achieve maturity, trim them in a similar fashion. This will enable a bonsai's branches to grow longer and more dense at the same time. Occasionally, due to plant disease or pests, only one branch will emerge from the bud.

Although trimming is a necessary part of the training process, one should not overdo it,

Many bonsai materials can be borrowed from nature. Make use of nature's gifts to indulge your creative spirit.

as it actually wounds the tree. Following each trimming, a bonsai needs time to heal and rehabilitate.

A bonsai with dense growths of tiny branches should produce small, delicate leaves. Leaves become smaller if there are relatively more of them. This is something to consider if one decides to trim a bonsai with the intent of creating more branch growth. Some bonsai, especially those with extraordinarily attractive leaves, should not be trimmed too much for the above reason.

Although pleasing to the eye, dense growths of tiny branches have disadvantages. In seasons of great heat or humidity, the

star jasmine / cascade style / height: 7cm(3 inches) / deep square high-waisted pot
mulberry / shari, twin-trunk / height: 7cm(3 inches) / bag-like pitch-black pot

mulberry / slanting-trunk / height:5cm (2 inches)/ hand-molded pot
mountain cherry / slanting-trunk / height:13cm(5 inches) / glazed earthenware pot

scarlet kadsura / coiled style / height: 15cm(6 inches) / round earthenware pot

Bonsai usually have small leaves and dense branches. The bonsai on this page, however, display sparse branches and large leaves. Try trimming branches and leaves in accordance with each tree's individual character.

branches and leaves near the trunk may not receive the proper amount of ventilation and sunlight, and may therefore wither, destroying the visual appeal of the bonsai. Thus, in order to guard against this, a cultivator must trim off all superfluous branches and check inner branches constantly to see if they are healthy.

gingko / tri-trunk / height:16cm (6.5 inches) / hand-molded earthenware pot

crape myrtle / slanting-trunk / height:5cm(2 inches) / rectangular outer-fringed pot
flowering quince / slanting-trunk/ height:6cm(2.5 inches) / hand-molded earthenware pot

Make use of a part that has not undergone layering to cultivate a broom style bonsai. For example, use new buds on the top of the plant which have sprouted after the plant was cut for layering purposes.

After the new buds grow as thick as a match, shape them with metal wires.

Bonsai Styles

I. Single - Trunk:

Upright style: Bonsai of this style have straight trunks that are thick near the base and tapered towards the top. To cultivate this style, cut the vertical roots of a young plant while encouraging the growth of its horizontal roots. In this way, it will have a strong root base to support its upward growth. Bonsai in this style look best when planted in wide, shallow vessels.

Coiled style: This is perhaps the simplest style for beginners to work with. It entails the shaping and twisting of a bonsai's trunk without any fixed pattern in mind. Use metal wire, props, or tiny ropes to bend the trunk into the desired shape.

Slanting style: Bonsai in the slanting style should lean to one side or the other. To ensure that the bonsai does not fall over, one should encourage the growth of a "support" root, which grows in alignment with the trunk of the bonsai, and a "tensile" root, which grows in an opposite direction.

Broom style: A bonsai in this style should have the appearance of an upside-down broom. To cultivate such a bonsai, first select a fairly mature bonsai with a well-developed root system and a relatively thick trunk. Next, cut off all the branches, leaving a simple, upright, flat-topped trunk. Treat the cut with a disinfectant, and wait for tiny buds to appear on the cut surface. When the buds emerge, pluck off all of them except for five or six evenly spaced ones. When the buds develop into thin branches, use wire to stretch them upward and outward. After they have matured somewhat, begin trimming each branch to promote the growth of smaller branches. Train all branches so that they stretch upward and outward.

From top to bottom:
azalea / exposed-root style / height:14cm(5.5 inches)/
round earthenware pot
star jasmine / rock-and-tree combination/
height:8cm(3 inches) / glazed oval earthenware pot
gingko / coiled style / height:13cm(5 inches)/
wheel-patterned earthenware pot
Chinese brake / clump style / height:7cm(3 inches)/
hand-molded earthenware pot
crape myrtle / upright style / height:
15cm(6 inches) / shallow oval pot

Chinese elm / twin-trunk/ height:8cm(3 inches) / pear-colored oval pot

This is a twin-trunk style formed by layering. Cut off from its mother plant only the previous year, the plant is quite little, with its root-base hardly visible.

green maple / twin-trunk/ height:34cm(13.5 inches)/ shallow oval pot

This twin-trunk bonsai was formed by layering after three years of cultivation. The growth of its root-base is readily apparent.

II. Double-trunk, tri-trunk, multi-trunk style:

In the double-trunk style, the trunks of two separate trees are grafted together to become one tree. Prepare both trees by removing the bark from the trunk of each tree at the point at which they will be joined. Bind the two trunks to one another so that the wounds can heal together. After about four months, the two trunks will be joined at the point where the wounds used to be. To blend three or more trunks, basically the same process is followed, but the time it takes for the joining to be complete ranges from six months to a year. To increase your chances of success, only the same species of tree when creating bonsai in this style.

III. Literati style:

This type of bonsai should be tall and slim. To keep such a bonsai stable, it is usually necessary to cultivate horizontal roots, or to use metal wires for support.

Japanese serissa / tri-trunk/ height:35cm(13 inches)/ shallow white-porcelain pot

Japanese serissa is excellent for exposed-root style bonsai. The tri-trunk style in the picture is the result of 20 years of cultivation.

cherry / cascade style / inner diameter of the pot:3cm(1.2 inches) / round bean-like pot

trident maple / cascade style / height:8cm (3 inches) / high-waisted purple-red pot

IV. Cascade style:

If cultivating a bonsai in this style, choose as your material something that is soft and easy to mold, such as a banyan, cypress or willow. Also suitable are creeping or trailing plants, such as bougainvillea, humid euphorbia, Chinese wisteria, or flowering quince.

If cultivating a cascade style bonsai from nursery stock, select one that is naturally slanted or twisted (the twisted section should be located only a little bit above the root-base).

Do not place a cascade style bonsai in a shallow or wide container. Instead use a tall, slim pot. Remember that the eventual living space for these bonsai is such a pot when you start pruning. Make sure to trim off horizontal roots, and to encourage the growth of vertical roots. In this way, the bonsai will fit into the pot.

As for how far down the trunk should droop when the bonsai is completed, that is up to the individual artist's preference. Training the trunk is a time consuming process. If one tries to create a bent trunk in too short a span of time, the bonsai may be

harmed. At the same time one is training the trunk downward, one can also train the branches to grow out with the help of metal wires. A completed cascade bonsai should feature a drooping trunk and horizontal branches.

A naturally occuring cascade style plant.

Japanese serissa / rock-and-tree combination / height of the rock: 5cm(2 inches) / round red pot

Chinese elm / rock-and-tree combination / height:12cm(5 inches)/ slabstone

V. Clinging-to-rock or root-over-rock style:

One of the most important tasks in completing one of these bonsai is to choose a suitable rock. Such a rock should have an interesting color, should be both dense and hard, and should be unevenly proportioned without being ungraceful. While roots have an easier time clinging to rocks which are soft and porous, such rocks have a tendency to break apart. Do not choose a rock with a slippery or completely smooth surface, because roots will not be able to attach themselves to it. Before using a rock from the beach or from near an ocean, carefully clean all vestiges of salt off of it.

Choose a plant or tree with vertically growing roots, clean off the soil surrounding the roots, and arrange the roots around the rock so that they fit into natural crevices and conform to the shape of the rock. Bind the roots and rock together with a soft hemp rope. Trim roots that are too long. Place the plant and rock in a container with porous soil covering the roots.

Let the tree grow naturally, pruning only those branches which grow out of control. Apply a small amount of potassic fertilizer to help the roots to grow. After one or two years, when the roots have grown tightly around the rock, trim the branches that are too long and remove the soil from the bottom of the rock to expose the roots for viewing purposes.

Japanese premna / rock-and-tree combination / height of the rock: 10cm(4 inches) / rectangular blue pot

When creating bonsai combined with rocks, make sure to choose rocks that match the shape of the roots. Every part of the tree in the picture, for example, clings closely to the rock except for the little space near the trunk. After one more year of cultivation, the space will fill in as the roots grow.

shrub althea / exposed-root style/ height:19cm(7.5 inches) / shallow oval pot

The exposed-root style of a tree cultivated in a seedbed.

The exposed-root style of trees in nature.

VI. Exposed-root style:

To cultivate this style of bonsai, first plant a small bonsai in a seed bed or in a large, deep container. Then, every so often, remove a layer of soil until the roots are gradually exposed. When the roots are exposed to the cultivator's liking, the bonsai is transplanted into a more permanent container.

Avoid undue haste in exposing the roots. If the soil removal is not carried out gradually, the roots will wither and die.

Exposed-root bonsai should feature roots that are exposed at least to the point where they connect with the main trunk of the tree. The deeper the roots are exposed, the better. Sometimes, these bonsai are eventually converted into root-over-rock bonsai.

Japanese premna / shari / height:
12cm(5 inches) / drum-like red pot

VII. Shari style:

Do not attempt to create bonsai in this style during hot or dry weather. If the weather is cool or humid, and one has selected a hardy material to work with, one can begin cultivating such a bonsai by first stripping a section of bark from the trunk of the tree. After the stripping is complete, apply disinfectant, such as a mixture of lime and sulfur, and then cover the wound with moss or linen fabric to prevent dehydration. Disinfection of the trunk must not be neglected. In humid weather, disinfect the trunk regularly to avoid the growth of mold.

Sometimes a bonsai artist will plant a tiny bonsai in the crook of a shari style bonsai. If this is one's intention, choose a strong and disease-free shari bonsai, so that the smaller bonsai does not become infected and die. In addition, be sure to select two bonsai that complement one another.

shrub althea / shari / height:20cm(8 inches)/ drum-like red pot

A naturally occuring example of the shari style.

103

VIII. Raft style

The point of this style is to encourage one root to give rise to two or more branches. Choose as a raw material Chinese fir, Chinese sweet gum, maple, beech, elm or banyan. Prepare the material by trimming off all the branches that grow downward or horizontally and all the roots that grow upward. With a knife, carve some grooves near the bottom of the trunk. Turn the trunk on its side, and apply to it some expanding-root fertilizer. Eventually, buds will emerge where the grooves were made. When this occurs, cut off overlong roots, and lay the trunk flat in a suitable container with soil covering it. With time, new branches will emerge from the earth. Prune off unwanted branches when necessary.

Taiwan red maple / raft style, twin-trunk/ height:21cm(8 inches) / shallow oval pot

white dragon grass / raft / height:14cm (5.5 inches) / bag-like oval pot

The best materials for raft style bonsai are creepers or species whose roots produce buds.

Japanese mountain maple / forest style / height:20cm(8 inches)/ stone piece

IX. Forest style:

A forest bonsai may be so large that it can only be moved by several people, or small enough to fit in the palm of one's hand. It usually features several small trees arranged so that they form a forest scene. All the trees placed together in a forest bonsai should complement each other and have similar growing patterns.

If one has several bonsai that aren't much to look at in themselves, they can be combined to form a forest style bonsai.

willow fir / forest style / height:21cm(8 inches) / bag-like oval pot

Fir is a species suitable for group planting. Before planting a fir in a shallow pot, make sure to sort out its root system, so that it will be able to stand firmly.

Plant a few slender and small trees together, bind them with metal wire, and tend them carefully.

After a year, the trees stick to each other and become a wonderful bonsai.

A few poor-looking banyans planted together in a pot can create a magnificent bonsai.

Rapid Cultivation

If one wishes to create a sturdy bonsai in a very short amount of time, the following method is one way of doing so: Take several slender, straight-growing seedlings with soft trunks and twist their trunks together just like a French braid. Plant them in a large pot, fertilize the soil abundantly, and shape them as quickly as possible. In time, the seedlings will naturally cling to one another and mature into a single bonsai with a thick, sturdy trunk.

After about a year, the braided seedlings are strong enough to move to a more permanent container. After they are shaped to the cultivator's liking, they will form an attractive bonsai. For beginners, Japanese serissa is perhaps the best material to use for this method of rapid cultivation.

When braiding, make use of the flexibility and shape of the trunks to wind them about one another, rather than relying on metal wires or rope. If one forces the braid to stay in place with rope or wire, as soon as the rope or wire is removed, the trees will come apart. In addition, they will bear the scars of the material used to hold them together.

Here is a cascade style plant cultivated in a seed-bed.

This little nursery stock looks more unique with the addition of thick moss.

Moss

Moss adds an additional visual element to a bonsai. Moss also protects soil from being washed or blown away, and slows the evaporation of water. For all these reasons, moss is an important part of bonsai cultivation.

Moss grows from spores. To cultivate moss, remove spores from naturally growing moss, strew them in a bonsai pot over soil, and cover them with damp cotton or tissue. After about two weeks, moss buds will begin to sprout, and after one year, there should be a lush growth of moss in the pot.

Frequently water moss as it has a tendency to dehydrate and wither. Do not apply fertilizer directly to moss. If one wishes to apply fertilizer to a bonsai combined with moss, the best way to do it is to squeeze the fertilizer into the soil from around the sides of the pot, or to lift up the layer of moss and spread fertilizer on the soil beneath it.

The moss should cover the soil evenly.

white dragon grass / raft style / height:
12cm(5 inches) / shallow wheel-patterned pot
star jasmine / cascade style / width:
6cm(2.5 inches) / square red pot
mulberry / cascade style / width:10cm(4 inches)/
square tall pot

Application
Bonsai Accessories

There is nothing more lovely than looking down upon a valley in which clumps of trees, broad meadows, and meandering rivers blend with tiny stone houses, wooden bridges, and other quaint traces of human habitation. Bonsai artists often strive to create a similar scene of beauty in their art works.

When arranging a bonsai in a pot, think of moss as a meadow. Place it next to clumps of tiny bonsai to create a forest scene. Rocks are often added to change the feel of a bonsai. Sharp jagged rocks conjure up images of a wasteland, and thus complement shari style bonsai. Brick fragments can be used as make-believe country paths winding through forest bonsai.

Miniature houses, bridges, pavilions, pagodas, human figures and animals are often added to bonsai. When purchasing such an accessory, choose only those made from pottery or stone, as wooden ones will mold in a damp environment, and plastic ones will ruin the naturalness of the scene.

When bonsai are displayed, they are often placed on a tiny table. Special multi-shelf cabinets are also available for displaying a number of bonsai at once. Never fill each shelf of such a cabinet, however, as it will then resemble a stock shelf rather than a piece of art.

Tiny bridges, huts and people for landscape bonsai.

Modern bonsai stands.

Bonsai rocks.

109

Su Tung-po (a well-known Chinese writer and artist) testing his new inkstone. A drawing by Wu Yu-lu. Ch'ing Dynasty.

Displaying Bonsai

A miniature bonsai, with its characteristic delicacy, is an ideal object for displaying indoors. When placing a bonsai in your home, keep the following in mind:

1. Sufficient sunlight is a must. All sides of a bonsai must receive an equal amount of sunlight, or the bonsai will grow unevenly.
2. Ventilation. A tree that is placed in an area where ventilation is poor will not respire as it should and will lose its luster. This does not mean to place bonsai in a windy area, or in front of the air-conditioner, however, as doing so will cause their leaves to dry up and wither.
3. Moderate temperature. Do not put a bonsai near any electrical device that produces heat.

An indoor environment is not entirely suitable for the cultivation of bonsai, so those bonsai placed indoors must be carefully monitored. In addition, one should place the bonsai outside for a few days about twice a month. The best thing to do is to rotate your bonsai so that they each spend some time outdoors as well as indoors.

When placing bonsai outdoors, it is easiest to put twenty or thirty of them on a medium-sized table so that they can be cared for all at once.

Large mountain rocks have no special displaying position. But since a wet environment can enhance the luster of the rock surface and the trees on it, a wide and shallow plate filled with water is recommended as a container.

(middle) banyan / group planting / height: 20cm(8 inches) / shallow round earthenware pot
(middle-right) Japanese privet / raft/ height:6cm(2.4 inches) / oblong earthenware pot

(right) Japanese serissa / root-over-rock/ rock height:5cm(2 inches) / hexagonal earthenware bowl

Here are some hints to keep in mind when placing bonsai outside:

1. Protect the bonsai from strong winds. Also, avoid placing them near air conditioner or air pump outlets.
2. Protect the bonsai from intense sunshine. One can use a sunshade net to reduce the amount of sunlight falling on the plants.
3. Choose a place for your bonsai that is not in the path of animals or children. In this way, unnecessary damage to the bonsai can be avoided.

bird-lime holly / cascade/ horizontal length:7cm(3 inches) / round earthenware bowl
mulberry / twisted-trunk/ height:8cm(3.2 inches)/ wide-mouthed square earthenware pot

An outdoor table is also a suitable place for displaying miniature bonsai.

fragrant maple / twin-trunk / height:8cm(3 inches) / shallow oval earthenware pot
common nandina / upright / height:16cm(6.5 inches) / tall square earthenware pot

Traditional Chinese tea sets are perfect for displaying next to bonsai. But keep hot pots or cups a distance away from the bonsai and do not water bonsai with tea as this will acidify the soil.

indigo plant / container length:20cm(8 inches) / handmade earthenware pot

To set bonsai near a window when no windowsill is available, use a hanging container. Creeping plants are most suitable for this method of display. Remember to take the container down when there is a strong wind.

112

shrub althea / cascade / horizontal length:16cm(6.5 inches) / tall square earthenware pot
white popinac / slanting / height:7cm(3 inches) / oblong earthenware pot

    Lighting can improve the appearance of bonsai. But do not place bonsai too close to the light source or the heat will do harm to the plant. Some plants, such as white popinac, will only close their flowers and rest in the dark. The constant light will thus mix up their bioclock and severly interfere with natural growth.

People often place bonsai on an indoor closet or shelf, which is not an ideal position because of a lack of sunshine. The plant should be set outdoors every couple days. If put in a closet, the closet door should be removed.

weeping willow / twisted-trunk / height: 17cm(7 inches) / round earthenware pot
mulberry / twisted-trunk / height:10cm(4 inches) / round glazed earthenware pot

Bonsai in a cascade style are usually placed on a shelf or the corner of a tabletop.

star jasmine / cascade / vertical length:5cm (2 inches) / earthenware jar
grape / shari / height:13cm(5 inches) / wide-mouthed square earthenware pot

oriental bittersweet / twisted-trunk / height:15cm(6 inches) / round earthenware pot
pomegranate / slanting / height:11cm(4.5 inches) / round earthenware pot
Japanese mountain maple / tri-trunk(5.5 inches) / height:14cm (5.5 inches) / handmade earthenware bowl

The development of Chinese bonsai is a product of the leisure activities of traditional Chinese literati. Chinese landscape painting and bonsai were two favorite hobbies of Chinese literati, so they go well together.

mulberry / shari / height:6cm(1.7 inches) / earthenware bowl
varnish tree / literati / square earthenware pot
crape myrtle / upright / height:10cm(4 inches) / wide-mouthed earthenware pot

Mirrors add another dimension to a bonsai scene. Set a delicate bonsai on your dressing table in front of a mirror.

忍氣免傷財
強暴必招災
巧處藏些獸
鄉黨要和諧
災退福星來

mulberry / cascade / horizontal length:10cm(4 inches) / tall square earthenware pot
five-leaved chaste-tree / twisted-trunk / height:18cm(7 inches) / round earthenware pot
trident maple / exposed-root / height:9cm(3.5 inches) / oblong earthenware pot
Displaying miniature bonsai among classic antiques creates an atmosphere of elegance.

(right) fragrant maple / twisted-trunk/
height:8cm(3 inches) / oblong earthenware
pot
(middle-right) Japanese serissa / exposed-
root / height:20cm(8 inches)/
shallow round earthenware pot
(left) Japanese red maple / semi-cascade/
horizontal length:20cm(8 inches)/
tall square earthenware pot
　　A table beside a window is an ideal place
for displaying bonsai.

white dragon grass / raft / height:13cm(5
inches) / handmade earthenware pot
　　Putting miniature bonsai on a desk in the
study can brighten up the room.

coconut / group planting / rock height:11cm(4.5 inches)/ shallow oval earthenware pot
Chinese break / multi-trunk / height:4cm(1.5 inches)/ handmade earthenware bowl

Tropical plants should be placed in a bright place to create a lively tropical atmosphere. Since tropical plants display strong positive phototropism, the position of such a bonsai should be adjusted from time to time to maintain balanced growth.

azalea / cascade / container height:17cm(7 inches) / round glazed earthenware pot
trident maple / cascade / container height:4cm(1.5 inches)/ rough-faced earthenware pot

Japanese style straw mats and rocks can create a simple and natural setting for bonsai.

large-leaf dogwood / cascade / vertical length:15cm(6 inches)/
handmade earthenware pot
varnish tree / upright / height:10cm(4 inches) / red earthenware tripod
dwarf stewartia / upright / height:21cm(8.5 inches) / handmade
earthenware pot

shrub althea / cascade / horizontal length:17cm(7 inches)/
round earthenware pot
Nagasaki crab-apple / upright / height:10cm(4 inches) / red earthenware tripod
Japanese premna / twisted-trunk / height:17cm(7 inches) / round
earthenware pot

When displaying bonsai, do not place them all in a straight line. You can arrang
them at several heights or in the form of an angle. Do not fill all the vacancies of a mut
shelf stand or it will look like a stock shelf.

119